D1214094

THE CONCEPT OF LANGUAGE

THE CONCEPT

OF

LANGUAGE

N. L. Wilson

UNIVERSITY OF TORONTO PRESS

Preface

A number of writers, in pursuing their investigations in what might loosely be called linguistic analysis, have found it convenient to work within the threefold framework of semiotic as set up by C. W. Morris.[1] At the lowest level of semiotic, that is, pragmatics, we are concerned with the language user and his use of signs to signify something. At the second level, semantics, we abstract from the use of a language, and concentrate on signs as signifying. In syntax, at the highest level of abstraction, we neglect even the external reference or signification of signs, and concern ourselves solely with the intralinguistic, syntactical relations holding among signs.

This work happens to be a study in general semantics. It runs the risk of appearing to be more difficult than it really is because it assumes in the reader some knowledge of technical philosophy. In particular it assumes the kind of familiarity with the techniques of symbolic logic that would come from working through a textbook such as Irving M. Copi's *Symbolic Logic.* In chapter III I have adopted Russell's theory of descriptions *in toto* and, perhaps mistakenly, I regarded it as too well known to require exposition. The interested reader is referred to Whitehead and Russell, *Principia Mathematica,* second edition, pages 67–71, for a discussion of descriptions and the use of scope symbols. He may be able to take some encouragement from the fact that there is scarcely any mention of descriptions in chapter v, the core chapter of this book. The basic aims and techniques of technical semantics present less difficulty and here one might claim that the book is for the most part self-contained. However, the reader interested in getting at background material could scarcely do better than to read the first eleven sections of Carnap's *Foundations of Logic and Mathematics* (see bibliography at the end of this book). Carnap's *Introduction to Semantics* is of course excellent but more difficult.

I wish to express my thanks to Routledge and Kegan Paul for permission to include a quotation from F. P. Ramsey's *Foundations of Mathematics* and to the director of the *Revue Internationale de Philosophie* for permission to quote from Carnap's article, "Empiricism, Semantics and Ontology." I am also grateful to the

---

[1] See his "Foundations of the Theory of Signs," *International Encyclopedia of Unified Science,* vol. I, no. 2 (Chicago, 1932). See also Carnap's *Introduction to Semantics,* Part A.

editor of *Mind* for his kind permission to include an altered version of my paper, "Existence Assumptions and Contingent Meaningfulness," and to the editors of the *Journal of Philosophy* and the *Philosophical Review* respectively for permission to use the substance and some of the phrasing of my papers, "Designation and Description," and "Property Designation and Description."

I am under a more intangible kind of debt to any number of people, but I should like to mention in particular the following. It was Professor Gordon Matheson, who, years ago when we were both graduate students, first put me onto the question, "What is a language?" Since then, I have had reason to be grateful to him for some stimulating correspondence arising out of one or two of my papers. Some of his suggestions have been incorporated into this book. Professor Rulon S. Wells read a primitive draft of this book and offered some excellent advice. I am more than grateful for the discussions we have had from time to time. I should also like to thank my colleague Professor Romane L. Clark for considerable help with the material in the Appendix.

I am indebted also to Professor and Mrs. Eric Yarrill of Bishop's University for their help with the German examples, to Mr. John Heintz for assisting me with the proofs and to Miss Elizabeth Ferrell for her assistance in preparing the index. Miss Barbara W. Ham, of the University of Toronto Press, performed with great care and good sense the task of seeing the manuscript through the press.

And finally, I should like to express my gratitude to the Canadian taxpayer, who, through the Department of Veterans' Affairs, underwrote the cost of most of my higher education and who, through the Canada Council and the Humanities Research Council of Canada, provided this book with a grant which made possible its publication. I should also like to acknowledge the assistance of the Publications Fund of the University of Toronto Press.

N. L. W.

Durham, North Carolina
January, 1959

Contents

THE CONCEPT OF LANGUAGE

I. CRITICAL

§1. INTRODUCTION

A book such as this might have been inspired by a feeling that after some fifty years during which philosophy has been regarded as the analysis of language, it is high time that we actually analysed *language*. I myself was not guided by so simple and cogent a thought. It was rather that more distant and complicated perplexities raised for me the question: What is a language?

The question itself is quite complicated and to effect a preliminary clarification I shall exploit the distinction Quine draws in his *Objects* between individuative terms (e.g., 'apple') and bulk terms (e.g., 'water').[1] Notwithstanding the restrictive connotations of the word 'individuative' I shall, in what follows, extend the use of both these terms to cover not just first order predicates, but also terms of higher order. It is a characteristic of individuative expressions as such that they may be used with an indefinite article or in the plural. It seems to be a characteristic of bulk terms as such that the same thing is *not* true of them. They are used without an indefinite article and never in the plural. We might say, "I had an apple for dessert," or, "I had apples for dessert," or "I had ice-cream for dessert." But we would never say, "I had apple for dessert," or "I had an ice-cream for dessert," or "I had ice-creams for dessert." There are, of course a whole host of bulk terms: 'gold', 'earth', 'air', 'flesh', 'bone', 'vinylite' and so on. We may describe the distinction in another way by saying that in the case of bulk terms it makes sense to ask, "How much?" whereas in the case of individuative terms the question would be, "How many?" Some terms double as both individuative and bulk terms. For example, we might have occasion to ask the questions, "How many bones did he break?" and, "How much bone did the surgeon remove?"

It is a characteristic of the word 'language' that, rightly or wrongly, it enjoys this kind of double use. When we say, "Philosophy is the analysis of language," or, "Language is the most characteristic product of the human race," we cast the word in the role of a bulk term. When we say, "He was using a language I did not understand," or

[1]Abbreviated titles will be used in the text, full bibliographical information being given in the list of references at the end of the book.

"Languages cannot contain mathematics and at the same time be both complete and consistent," we are using 'language' as an individuative term—in an extended sense of 'individuative'. I may say at once that this double use of the word 'language' seems to me to be a mistake. (Incidentally, the same observation could be made on the word 'substance'.) It makes sense to ask, "How many languages are spoken in Switzerland?" but it does not make sense to ask, "How much language is spoken in Switzerland?" unless perhaps the question means, "How loquacious are the Swiss?" (The question, "How much French does he know?" if it means anything at all, must mean something like, "How large a sub-language of French has he mastered?")

We may conclude, I think, that the word 'language' has a clear and correct use only as an individuative term. At least this would seem to be its primary use. And in saying that I shall attempt to analyse the concept of language, I wish to make it clear that I am not asking the question, "What is language?" (Cf. "What is vinylite?") Rather, I am asking, "What is *a* language?" (Cf. "What is a cyclotron?") The question, "What is vinylite?" is of course a perfectly good question, but there is no comparable kind of question in the case of languages, because a language is a thing or entity of a certain kind, it is not a kind of stuff or a piece of stuff. Strictly speaking, this book should be entitled "The Concept of Languagehood," languagehood being the property of being a language. The barbarism 'languagehood' would permit us to distinguish clearly the present enterprise from that of defining a particular language, the sort of thing Carnap does in his *Semantics*. Of course once we acquire convictions as to the nature of languagehood, these will issue in a fairly elaborate set of opinions as to how one ought to go about defining any specific language.

In this work I shall also be concerned to do a large-scale White-Quine. Morton G. White and W. V. Quine (in *Dualism* and *Dogmas* respectively) have claimed that they do not understand the word 'analytic', or at least that they do not see that a sharp distinction between analytic and synthetic has been formulated. I have to confess to being much duller than these writers. In the beginning at least, I do not understand the broad term 'analytic', nor do I understand the narrower term 'logically true'. And I do not even understand the terms 'true' and 'designates'. And I should contend that nobody else understands these terms either. For convenience I shall refer to these as 'the semantic terms'. However, in most cases I know what I want in the way of clarifications. The book is thus divided into three unequal parts: critical (a listing of three very general complaints in the remainder of this chapter), constructive (two complaints taken care of in chapters II–VI), and programmatic (methods suggested for dealing with the third in chapter VII). It should not be surprising that an investigation of the nature of languages should provide some clarification of the semantic terms, since they are all two- or three-place predicates taking language names or variables as one of their arguments.

The word 'analytic' is a broad term covering not only logically true (provable) sentences and true Gödelian sentences, but also certain sentences in which descriptive expressions occur essentially. In the sentence, 'All brothers are brothers', the word 'brothers' may be replaced by any other expression of the same logical type, and the truth value of the sentence will be unchanged. Thus 'brothers' does not occur essentially in the given sentence—it occurs *vacuously*. On the other hand, if in the true sentence, 'All brothers are male', the word 'brothers' is replaced by 'sisters', we get a false sentence, showing that 'brothers' does occur essentially in the latter sentence. Analytic sentences containing descriptive expressions essentially will be referred to as 'descriptively analytic'. Analytic sentences containing defined and defining expressions essentially seem to me to be less interesting than those descriptively analytic sentences like 'Tully is identical with Cicero' and 'Red is between orange and purple', in which only *primitive* descriptive expressions occur. There is a question indeed as to whether these latter really are analytic. At any rate the problem of descriptive analyticity is quite subtle (particularly in regard to the second class) and will receive scarcely more than passing notice in chapter VII.

In order to explain what I shall *not* be doing in this book it is necessary to have a distinction between explication and definition. In a philosophical analysis we start with a vague pre-analytic concept (or what Carnap calls an *explicandum*[2]) which is connected somehow with certain philosophical perplexities. The pre-analytic concept has a certain definiteness in so far as we have certain habits in using the name of the concept. In analysis we seek to arrive at an explicit definition of a new concept. Both the definiendum and the definiens refer to the new concept, what Carnap calls the *explicatum*. There is no question of the pre-analytic concept being identical with the explicatum because the former is vague whereas the latter is articulate. But the explicatum offers itself as a replacement of the pre-analytic concept in the sense that our new definition may accommodate in large measure our pre-analytic use of the term in question, and at the same

[2]See Carnap's excellent discussion in §2 of his *Probability*.

time offer an explicit rationale for that use. And it may decide questions of application of the term which, at the pre-analytic level, were in doubt. For example, suppose we are worried about the concept of causation. We have some kind of pre-analytic concept of *cause* in so far as we say things like 'Lightning causes thunder', 'Yellow fever is caused by bacteria'. But we may be in doubt as to whether we ought to say, "Smoking causes lung cancer." The philosophical analysis presumably issues in an explicit definition of the word 'cause'. We have a new concept but our definition will still permit us to say that lightning causes thunder. Furthermore, it makes it clear why we say that lightning causes thunder. And although our definition will not tell us whether smoking causes lung cancer, it will indicate the kind of circumstance which would justify us in saying that it does and the kind of circumstance that would justify us in saying that it does not.

Now in philosophical analysis we may have this kind of situation: We have a pre-analytic concept, P, and we lay down an explicit definition of 'P'. It may be that the defined concept is recognizably distinct from the pre-analytic concept—not in being less vague but in being in a sense more vague. It might be that the definition leaves in doubt certain applications of 'P' which were not at all in doubt at the pre-analytic level. Nevertheless we might be justified in calling our new concept 'P' if it bears to the pre-analytic concept a certain peculiar relation which can be characterized in the following way: It is possible, without altering the definition, to introduce supplementary definitions and thereby transform our new concept into something sufficiently like the old. *With* the supplementary definitions our original definition of 'P' is now an explication of P. For example, Peano's system defined '0', '1', '2', etc.—'0' implicitly by the axioms, the others by explicit definition. (I am regarding an axiom set as a kind of definition.) But the system does not explicate our pre-analytic concepts of the numbers 0, 1, 2, etc., as the system of Whitehead and Russell does. For Peano's system provides us with no analyses of descriptive sentences like 'There are nine planets'. To put the point another way, we may say that Peano's system admits of non-normal interpretations. The entities in its domain might be taken to be all the even numbers plus 0, or all the numbers from one hundred up. But suppose we supplemented Peano's language with descriptive terms and added axioms governing the joint use of descriptive and arithmetic expressions. Now our augmented set of axioms and definitions would presumably not merely define the numerals but would also explicate our pre-analytic concepts of the numbers. I have used the example of explicating number concepts because the procedure suggested is what is to be followed in the Appendix, where a new approach to cardinal arithmetic is required. And something like this procedure is envisaged for the concept of language and the semantic concepts.[3] We have an illustration of the general methodological principle: in the case of important philosophical concepts, you have not explicated *anything* until you have explicated a great deal else besides. This principle has the discouraging consequence that philosophical analysis has to be done in large chunks.

The misgivings I expressed earlier regarding the semantic terms may now be put more bluntly. There exist no explications of the semantic terms and *there do not exist even general working definitions for semantics comparable to Peano's working definitions for arithmetic*. This book aims at supplying general definitions, but full explications will not be achieved. I am taking 'full explication' in a rather strong sense. A concept is fully explicated if the term in question can be eliminated from *all* important contexts. Obviously this kind of full explication of the concept of language and of the semantic terms can only be accomplished in pragmatics. The present book is an essay in general semantics only.

The following remarks have to do with the lacuna just mentioned. Philosophical activity may begin under one of at least two conditions. The philosopher is confronted with a problem. He has a definiendum (or if you like, an explicandum) for which he is seeking a definiens. (For example, the problem of finding a definiens for 'If x were . . . then x would be . . . '.) On the other hand a philosopher may be perplexed or dissatisfied. He has no definiendum and his task is that of finding one which somehow "fits" his perplexity. (For example, Nelson Goodman in writing *Counterfactuals* was presumably perplexed about physical laws and finally decided that 'If x were . . . then x would be . . . ' is a definiendum appropriate to his dissatisfaction.) If we characterize philosophy as the business of analysing concepts in the sense of finding definientia, then we run the risk of representing philosophical analysis as being rather more trivial than it really is. For this account totally ignores the important and sometimes exceedingly difficult matter of finding systematically fruitful definienda which either fit perplexities we *do* have or fit perplexities we ought to have. To suffer from perplexity over existence, to recognize that a distinction between existence and non-existence is *not* an appropriate definiendum

[3]This kind of procedure is suggested by Carnap, *Syntax*, p. 229.

and that a distinction between categorematic and syncategorematic expressions does at least in part fit the perplexity, is an activity of a different order from that of actually elaborating the latter distinction (that is, finding the definiens). At present we have no definiendum which matches our perplexity about the relation between mind and body, and on that account we are sometimes tempted to conclude that there is no problem there. On the other hand, if a writer wishes to maintain that there *is* a problem involving something or other, then about the only way he can make out his case is to produce the definiendum. The difficulty, of course, is that our perplexities usually have a certain objective order, and they can only be resolved in that order. But in the beginning we are too perplexed to recognise that order. That is why philosophical activity is in part rather like trying to find the end of a tangled skein of wool.

Chapter VII contains a discussion of the alleged natural language–artificial language distinction and from it we arrive at three definienda containing the word 'uses'. These are the *fundamental definienda of pragmatics* and they in a sense define a programme. If appropriate definientia were supplied (and offhand at least, there would not seem to be insuperable difficulties) then these definitions (as supplementary) together with the definitions of chapter V of this work would presumably constitute a system in which all the semantic concepts would be explicated.[4]

Before we proceed it is necessary to introduce a disavowal. In attempting to answer the question, 'What is a language?' we shall be seeking a general definition of the word 'language'. Lest the contents of this book be falsely advertised in the introduction I should mention the limits to the generality of the definition we shall finally arrive at. For one thing, the definition will not cover the metalanguage. Considerations dealt with by Tarski in his *Wahrheitsbegriff* would lead us not to expect a general definition of language covering the metalanguage *in which* the definition is formulated. Again, it covers languages only of the standard symbolic types, not languages of the type of used languages. Moreover, it is found necessary to use a metalanguage of a rather special kind; it is neither extensional nor intensional. And it is found convenient to suppose that all the object languages are of the same kind logically as the non-semantical parts of the metalanguage. And it goes without saying that we shall be interested only in the cognitive aspects of languages. But for all its clear limitations we shall at least have a general definition which will satisfy certain

---

[4]Actually, I wonder if the semantic concepts will be fully explicated until a complete system of semiotic is geared in with a complete system of confirmation theory.

criteria of adequacy, be sufficiently articulate to save us from confusion, and permit us to use the locution, 'For every language L . . . ', with a clear idea of what the variable 'L' ranges over. And by an intuitive extrapolation of the definition we can gain some insight into the nature of languages in general.

Since the present account of language has been inspired largely by a study of Carnap's writings, I shall begin by mentioning the difficulties to be encountered in his *Semantics*. The first concerns the notion of a semantical system as constituted by its rules. The second centres around the definitions of the semantic terms and the difficulty of eliminating them. The third, which may be called 'the pedagogical difficulty', is of a different order. It has to do with use of a language and the semanticist can dismiss it as raising issues lying outside his province. Nevertheless it shows how very abstract a discipline semantics is.

§2. THE DIFFICULTY WITH RULES-AS-CONSTITUTIVE

"By a *semantical system* . . . ," Carnap writes (*Semantics*, p. 22), "we understand a system of rules, formulated in a metalanguage and referring to an object language. . . . " These rules, which are sentences of the metalanguage, define 'sentence in S', 'designates in S' and 'true in S'. Now if 'S' is the name of a system of rules, it is perhaps the name of the conjunction of rules or the class of rules. Whatever the case, it is clear that 'S' would be *meta*metalinguistic and could not appear *in* the metalinguistic rules. If, on the other hand, by 'rules' we understand, not sentences of the metalanguage, but rather what the sentences in question express, then 'S' is not the name of the conjunction of sentences in question but an abbreviation of their conjunction. But now the phrase 'designates in S' is still nonsense, for it contains an expression which is an abbreviation of a set of sentences containing 'designates in S' itself. Since the conception of a semantical system seems to be incoherent, I shall abandon it and allow the object language to assume the function of a semantical system. That is, I shall speak of *designation in L_1* and *truth in L_1*, where 'L_1' refers to the object language and not to the system of rules. *The rules are definitive of a language, they are not constitutive of it.* The procedure here is by no means novel, and in fact Carnap himself writes, "S_1 (that is to say, the object language of S_1) . . . ," a locution which suggests that he senses on p. 23 that all is not quite as it should be on p. 22. Now, however, we shall have to wonder what kind of thing the object language L_1 is.

§3. THE DOUBLE ELIMINATION DIFFICULTY

I shall begin with designation. It is not certain whether Carnap is (i) defining a unitary two-place predicate 'designates-in-L_1' (that is, 'Des$_{s_1}$', see *Semantics*, p. 50) or (ii) offering a partial contextual definition of a three-place predicate '. . . designates . . . in . . . ', that is, defining 'designates' *for* a given language L_1. (See *Semantics*, p. 25.)

(i) In the first case, since 'designates-in-L_1' is a unitary expression, it will not be possible to replace 'L_1' in it by a variable 'L' any more than we can replace the '6' in '64' by a numerical variable. And if this replacement cannot be made, then it will not be possible to arrive at a general definition of designation. (It might be noted that if the language rules contain these hyphenated semantic terms then the objection of §2 to using 'L_1' *by itself* as a name of a system of rules falls.) But it is difficult to see that these two-place predicates 'designates-in-L_1', 'designates-in-L_2' are of any interest.[5] Moreover we should presumably be involved in a series of one-place hyphenated truth concepts, 'true-in-L_1', 'true-in-L_2', etc., and we should be deprived of resources for saying, "A sentence may be true in one language and false in another."

(ii) The difficulty in the second case is this: If the language is somehow or other fully specified, which is to say that the characteristics by which it differs from other languages are given, then there is no objection to defining relations for that language. But a language is not fully specified, or given, or defined, apart from its designation rules. That is, if we try to define 'designates' for L_1 (that is, define the non-unitary phrase 'designates in L_1') then a person might legitimately ask, "Which language is the language L_1 for which you are defining 'designates'?" We should have to answer that it is a language in which —among other things—'a' designates Chicago. If the answer is to convey anything, then 'designates' must be antecedently understood.

The complaint here is essentially an objection against the practice of trying to define two new terms, 'designates' and 'L_1' by a single enumerative and possibly recursive definition. But perhaps this uneasiness at the attempt to define two terms at once is ill-founded. The normal requirement for a definition is that it should permit the elimination of the defined term. (This requirement might be too stringent in the case of recursive definitions but since any difficulties connected

---

[5] *Cf.* Quine on 'analytic-for-L_0', *Dogmas*, p. 32, second full paragraph, or *LPV*, p. 33, third paragraph.

with recursion are not to the point here, we shall suppose that 'designates' means 'directly designates'.) In special semantics the elimin-
ability requirement *is* satisfied. The word 'designates' always occurs
with a language name and they can presumably be eliminated together. Language names always occur with 'designates' or some other
semantic term (for example, 'true') which is defined in terms of
'designates', and again the joint elimination of terms would be possible.
I dislike the necessity of this double elimination but I am prepared
to concede that the objection here has weight only if we can find contexts where language names and semantic terms do not occur together and are therefore not eliminable.

We do not have to look far. The sentences, 'Walter Scott used L_1
in writing *Waverley*' and 'Walter Scott used "Auld Reekie" to designate Edinburgh' would serve, but by reason of the occurrence in them
of the word 'used', they raise issues of a separate kind, which I should
prefer to deal with in the next section. But in general semantics there
presumably occurs the phrase 'designates in L' ('L' a variable) and
'designates' would not be eliminable. In general semantics we should
have to take 'designates' as primitive. This would mean that we have
not even defined 'designates', let alone explicated *designation*.

I am calling for a general definition of designation, a demand comparable to a demand for a general definition of truth. It will be said
that this is asking too much. We do not have a definition of 'S is true
in L' for variable 'S' and variable 'L'. All we have is 'true' defined for
certain specific formalized language systems. But under these circum-
stances we have perhaps been too hasty in regarding the problem of
truth as finally settled. A scrutiny of this curious notion of *defining
for* might serve to shake our complacency.

Suppose we wish to define 'soluble (in water)' *for* those objects
which happen to be in water and, out of sheer laziness, we do not
wish to define it for any other objects. We try:

$$x \text{ is soluble } =_{\mathrm{df}} x \text{ is in water and } x \text{ dissolves.}$$

This will not do because it makes all objects not in water not
soluble. We try:

$$x \text{ is soluble } =_{\mathrm{df}} x \text{ is in water } \supset x \text{ dissolves.}$$

This will not do because on the usual interpretation of '$\supset$' it makes
all objects not in water soluble. And so we use Carnap's reduction
sentence:

$$x \text{ is in water } \supset (x \text{ is soluble } \equiv x \text{ dissolves}).$$

This sentence makes 'soluble' meaningless if applied to objects not in water, in the sense that it would not be possible to eliminate 'soluble' from the sentences making the application. But it is to be noted that 'soluble' from first to last is a one-place predicate.

Now 'true' is a two-place predicate and we shall wish a general definition of 'S is true in L' for variable 'S' and variable 'L' *for precisely the same reason that no matter how lazy we intend to be in defining 'soluble' we shall want some kind of definition of* 'x *is soluble' for variable* 'x'. Suppose we wish to define 'true' for just those languages having the property P. Then our definition would take the form:

$$P(L) \supset S \text{ is true in } L \equiv \ldots .$$

We should have at least some kind of *general* definition of truth. Properties which would not be acceptable in defining a restricted class of languages for which 'true' is to be defined are the L-determinate language properties like *the property of being identical with* L_1 *or identical with* L_2 *or* . . . with corresponding enumerative sections in the dotted portion of the definition schema given. They would not be acceptable because we ought to be able to do better than that. And it should be noted that even if, out of sheer, utter laziness, we were to define 'soluble' for just the individuals a, b, and c, then at least the names 'a', 'b', and 'c' are understood independently of our definition and we should presumably be able to arrive at a definition which would not require the double elimination noted earlier in the case of 'designates' and 'L_1'. (The definition of 'true' in chapter v is not of the form given above, because, as has already been admitted, the definition of 'language' will be such that the range of 'L', although infinite, will already have been restricted sufficiently to make it not too difficult to frame a definition of truth for all the values of 'L'.)

The point here is that it is in order to demand a general definition of 'true' and that it is equally in order to demand a definition in general semantics of the three-place predicate 'designates'. Carnap (in *Semantics*, p. 50) offers the following definition of truth:

D12-1. $\mathfrak{S}_i$ is *true* in $S =_{\mathrm{df}}$ there is a (proposition) p such that $\mathrm{Des}(\mathfrak{S}_i, p)$ and p.

I should suggest first of all that, assuming 'S' in the definiendum to be a variable ranging over Carnap's systems or our languages, we replace '$\mathrm{Des}(\mathfrak{S}_i, p)$' by '$\mathrm{Des}(\mathfrak{S}_i, p, S)$'. But even now the definition cannot be accepted because we have no general definition of the three-place predicate 'Des' occurring in the definiens. In chapter v such a definition will be offered, but by reason of certain necessary idiosyncrasies of the method (non-recognition of molecular and general propositions) it will not immediately yield a general definition of truth after the manner of D12-1.

Now to go back a bit. (1) We started by objecting to the practice of trying to define two new expressions, 'designates' and a language name, by one definition. (2) We noted that the objection would hold only if there are contexts containing just one of the new terms. (3) We found that 'designates in L' is such a context, one moreover for which it is reasonable to demand a definition. (4) We may conclude that the original objection to defining two terms at once was well taken. We thus have no general definition of 'designates', *a fortiori* no general definition of 'true' and *a fortiori* no general semantic definition of 'logically true', much less explications.

And even if, for *logical truth*, we retreat into syntax we encounter the same kind of difficulty.[6] The initial rules are supposed to define both a certain calculus K_1 *and* the phrase 'direct consequence' for that calculus. We should have no general definition of 'direct consequence' for general syntax and no general definition of the two-place predicate 'logically true' ('analytic' in the context of Carnap's *Syntax*). And it is just as reasonable to require such a definition of 'logically true' as it is to require a general definition of 'true'. Carnap's procedure in Part IV of his *Syntax* is somewhat curious. On p. 169 he writes, "We will assume the definition of 'direct consequence' to be stated in the following form . . . ." Thus where we should expect Carnap in general syntax to be dealing with an unspecified calculus, we find him instead dealing with unspecified rules—which takes us back to the objections against regarding rules as constitutive rather than as definitive.

The general kind of difficulty raised in this section might be put in a different way. The rules are supposed to specify the meanings which the various object language signs have in that language. (Isn't that what we should mean by saying that the rules define the language? *Cf.* Carnap, *Syntax*, p. 258: ". . . I prefer to regard the connection from the opposite direction, the relations of meaning between sentences are given by means of the rules of consequence.") And the rules are also supposed partially to define various semantical or syntactical terms. The rules are thus supposed to do two things at once and they simply cannot be expected to do both successfully. I am not happy

[6] I think Quine is raising it in his *Dogmas*, p. 32, first full paragraph, or *LP V*, p. 33, second paragraph.

about this way of putting the case, because I am not certain as to whether the difficulty as so formulated belongs in this section with the *curable* ills of semantics and syntax or in §4 with the incurable ills—those requiring pragmatic treatment. I infer from my uncertainty that it is not altogether clear what the difficulty as so stated is, and I am reasonably certain the unclarity is localized in the word 'meaning'. And so I shall drop the matter and assume that the complaint here will sooner or later succeed in getting itself lodged.

§4. THE PEDAGOGICAL DIFFICULTY

This difficulty is related to the double elimination difficulty, and in fact the discussion will appear at first glance to be a rehash of the preceding. But it is a distinct difficulty because it revolves around special semantics rather than general. Moreover, in chapter v the second difficulty will be taken care of, but I shall at most suggest a pure pragmatic programme for dealing with the present one. The somewhat heroic contention that *nobody* understands (philosophically) any of the terms 'analytic', 'logically true', 'true', 'designates' and 'language' receives perhaps its most telling defence in this section.

We shall suppose I am trying to teach a German (whom for convenience I shall call 'Hermann') the language L_1, which is in fact a suitably accurate reconstruction of English. (My reasons for *not* saying that I am teaching him English will become apparent in chapter VII.) I have a rule book for L_1 written in the manner of Carnap's *Semantics*. The book is written in English and so I shall have to translate parts of it into German for Hermann's benefit. But of course I shall not translate any *defined* word ('designates', 'true') into German, for if the definition is adequate I should not have to. I turn out to be a very bad teacher.

(i) I commence with the enumerative definition of 'designates' for L_1, telling Hermann, " 'Cologne' designates in der Sprache L_1 Köln; 'the moon' designates in der Sprache L_1 den Mond," and so on. In what sense can it be said that I am defining 'designates' or even 'L_1'? Hermann does not understand 'designates' when I start. When I have finished he perhaps understands it as referring to an arbitrary relation in extension, but he certainly does not know how to speak English. If, however, in the rules of L_1, instead of using 'designates', which Hermann does not understand, I had used 'bedeutet', which he does understand, then in principle at least, I could have taught him to use the atomic sentences of L_1 (that is, English). (By 'understand', I mean here 'has a casual working understanding', I do not mean that he has the kind of understanding philosophers are seeking.) On the other hand, since Hermann already knows what language German is, if I had told him, " 'Köln' designates auf Deutsch Köln; 'der Mond' designates auf Deutsch den Mond," and so on, I could presumably have conveyed to him that 'designates' means the same as 'bedeutet'. We may conclude that in a different sense from that discussed in §3, semantics as presently conceived fails to define 'designates' and fails to define its languages.[7]

(ii) Nor does it define 'true'. By relenting just a bit and using 'bedeutet' I have taught Hermann the meanings of primitive descriptive expressions of L_1, and by statements like "Der Satz 'the moon is yellow' ist *true* in der Sprache L_1 wenn und nur wenn der Mond gelb ist," I have conveyed to him that *for atomic sentences* the semantic concept of truth is the same as his pre-analytic concept of *Wahrheit*. Now suppose I try to teach him the meanings of the connectives of L_1 by means of rules of truth: "Ein Satz '*A* or *B*' ist *true* wenn und nur wenn '*A*' *true* ist oder '*B*' *true* ist." Since Hermann does not understand 'true' for molecular sentences, this statement does not convey to him the meaning in L_1 of 'or'. It might be that in L_1 sentences of the form '*A* or *B*' are conjunctions instead of disjunctions and *provided this fact could be antecedently established* the rule would then define a semantic concept of truth differing from Hermann's pre-analytic concept of *Wahrheit*. The point is that the rules of truth may be either contextual interpretations of the connectives or a partial definition of 'true'. They cannot be both at the same time. And so I have to relent a little more: by telling Hermann, "Ein Satz '*A* or *B*' ist wahr in L_1 wenn und nur wenn '*A*' wahr in L_1 ist oder '*B*' wahr in L_1 ist," I presumably convey to him the meaning in L_1 of 'or'.

(iii) There is another way. First I invoke 'bedeutet' again: "In L_1 wenn '*A*' die mögliche Tatsache dass p bedeutet und '*B*' die mögliche Tatsache dass q bedeutet, dann bedeutet der Satz '*A* or *B*' die mögliche Tatsache dass p oder q." Then we lay down the already mentioned rule of truth for atomic sentences and add the following: " '*A* or *B*' ist *true* in L_1 wenn und nur wenn '*A*' *true* in L_1 ist oder '*B*' *true* in L_1 ist." Here by the extensive use of the non-systematic word 'bedeutet' we can interpret 'or' and *then* define 'true' for L_1.

---

[7]Wilfrid Sellars has, I think, recognized the difficulty in §VII of his "Empiricism and Abstract Entities," to appear in the forthcoming volume, *The Philosophy of Rudolf Carnap*, edited by Paul A. Schilpp, The Library of Living Philosophers, Inc.

(iv) And there is the syntactical method. We tell Hermann, "In L_1 ist der Satz '*A* or *B*' *derivable* von dem Satz '*A*' und von dem Satz '*B*'." Since 'derivable' means nothing to Hermann we again have to relent and use 'ableitbar', which he does understand informally.[8] By doing so we succeed in interpreting 'or' in L_1 (and similarly the other logical signs) and can now go on to give an enumerative and recursive definition of 'true'.[9]

In all the foregoing, I have assumed that Hermann is a bit slow on the uptake. This is a legitimate gambit because in doing systematic analysis we write as if we were spelling things out for an audience with more patience than brains. We do so, because, in general, we are interested in systematic completeness and articulateness, and from that standpoint, a gap is a gap. The fact that Hermann might be clever enough to make an intuitive leap across the gap is not at all to the point. And if he is that clever, it is undoubtedly because we have used the non-systematic word 'Sprache' in our instructions. The necessity of relenting in one way or another, of relinquishing the defined jargon of semantics for the understood but unanalysed terms of Hermann's ordinary German, shows that semantics supplies us with no explications. The rules of the customary sort are not such as to justify Carnap in writing (*Foundations L & M*, pp. 10–11), "We shall say that we understand a language system, or a sign, or an expression, or a sentence in a language system, if we know the rules of the system."

But of course any of us reading Carnap's *Semantics* does understand the signs of the system S_1. That is because we smuggle into the book sections of our pre-analytic concepts which have not been explicated in the book itself. It is as if someone had said to Hermann, "Hint: For 'designates' read 'bedeutet'." I do not wish to suggest *here* that there is anything wrong with semantics. There is no point in reproaching semantics for not being pragmatics. I am merely suggesting that semantics is more highly abstract than we may have realized. The semanticist's treatment of languagehood is not such as to conform to the following convention:

C1. A person knows what a certain language is (knows the identity of that language, understands, knows the meanings of the expressions of that language, understands the name of that language) if and only if he knows how to use that language.

[8]*Cf.* Quine, *Dogmas*, p. 32, first full paragraph.
[9]I should not be prepared to claim that *all* semantical methods are subject to *all* the difficulties mentioned. Yet I should hold that any method, if it is genuinely semantical, must be subject to the pedagogical difficulty.

This convention will only be used negatively in this book, because my own semantic methods will obviously not satisfy it. (The convention is, of course, a pragmatic one.) But the definitions offered in chapter v of this work will appear paradoxical and obviously wide of the mark. But it has now been shown that if the methods are inadequate, they are not less adequate than current methods, but only *more obviously* inadequate. One merit of the method is perhaps that it exhibits its poverty in so frank and unashamed a manner that it will be relatively easy to see what has yet to be done.

Two methods of conforming to C1 suggest themselves. We might seek to define 'language' in such a way that every language will come with built-in instructions for use. This seems so unpromising a possibility that I shall prefer to define 'language' apart from C1 and then call for (not provide here) general instructions for the use of any language. These would be the supplementary definitions mentioned in §1.

In (ii), (iii), and (iv) above three methods of dealing with the logical connectives were suggested. The first is not open to us, because in the beginning we shall not have a definition of 'true.' The second is not open to us because we find weighty reasons for renouncing molecular and general propositions. Our methods then will have to be generally similar to those used in (iv). That is to say, we shall borrow from both Carnap's *Syntax* and his *Semantics*. If I were to permit myself current ways of speaking (with which I am not altogether satisfied) I should put the matter in this way: To construct a language we first construct an uninterpreted descriptive calculus (a calculus containing non-logical constants) in which the meanings of the logical signs are presumably fixed by a list of primitive sentences and one or more rules of direct derivation. Then we supply designation rules to interpret the non-logical constants. Then we may go on to define 'true' for that language, in such a way that only true sentences are derivable from true sentences.

II. CRITERIA OF ADEQUACY

§5. THE NECESSITY
OF A DEFINITION OF 'LANGUAGE'

In §2 of chapter I we found what seemed to be a serious difficulty in treating a language as a system of rules. What then is a language? But before proceeding it might be as well to ask if the foregoing is a good question. Generally, the best way of showing that some question is a good one is to provide an interesting answer. But even at this stage we can provide some antecedent assurance that what is to follow is not merely busy-work.

A consideration of the double elimination difficulty would lead us to look for a method of specifying or defining a language apart from the semantic terms. The discovery of a general method would amount to the discovery of a general definition of 'language'. The foregoing argument is persuasive. The following is perhaps decisive.

We shall want to use language variables in general semantics, because we shall want to make statements about all languages and about some language. And in chapter VII it will be shown that the alleged language names 'English', 'French', 'Japanese', etc. are really abbreviations for language descriptions, which contain an iota operator with a variable 'L'. And since we must use language variables we shall have to ask: What are the values of these variables? What are the common characteristics of these values? Now it will be said that these are foolish questions. After all, we use individual variables, yet if we were to ask for the common characteristics of all the values of an individual variable we should find that their only common property is the property of being an individual, which is a universal property.

In order to find a reply to the foregoing, let us suppose we want a language with a variable 'c' to range over a restricted domain containing all and only cities. To effect this restriction, we should require, extrasystematically, a definition of 'city'. The use of such a restricted variable is exactly comparable to the use of '$(c)(\ldots)$' and '$(\exists c)(\ldots)$' as respective abbreviations for '$(x)(x$ is a city $\supset \ldots)$' and '$(\exists x)(x$ is a city $\& \ldots)$'. And to establish intrasystematic definitions of the restricted quantifiers we should require, intrasystematically, a definition of 'city'. It is assumed that we should not be content to take 'city' as primitive. Now the question is this: Apart from type differences, is '*L*' like '*x*' or is it like '*c*'? Is 'language' like 'individual' or is it like 'city'? If 'language' were like 'individual' we should expect to see *language* displayed prominently in the hierarchy of types along with *individual, first order first degree property* and all the rest. But we do not. And so we may conclude that 'language' is like 'city', and that just as 'What is a city?' is a good question which becomes urgent as soon as we propose to use a variable ranging over all and only cities, so also 'What is a language?' is a good question *which becomes urgent* as soon as we propose to use a variable ranging over all and only languages. (In a metalanguage whose variables are typeless, 'All languages are . . . ' would be rendered as '$(x)(x$ is a language $\supset \ldots)$' and a definition of 'language' would be just as much to the point.) Our problem in chapter v will thus fall into two unequal parts, the problem of deciding on a type for languages and the rather more difficult problem of finding a definition by which to classify the entities of that type into languages and non-languages.

§6. A FIRST CRITERION OF ADEQUACY

In this matter of finding a definition to differentiate languages from non-languages of the same type, we shall do well to have a criterion of adequacy to guide us. As a matter of fact, it will do no harm to have a criterion of adequacy for any criterion of adequacy. Convention C2 is what might be called 'the intercommunication requirement'.

C2. Two persons use the same language if and only if, in conversing about ordinary non-recondite matters, they succeed in exchanging information.

In calling C2 a criterion of adequacy for any criterion of adequacy, I mean simply that any criterion of adequacy chosen must guarantee in advance that any final definition of 'language' will be such as to permit us to assert C2. It is, of course, exceedingly imprecise, but the main thing is that it is precise enough to enable us to do with it what we want to do, namely, defend C3. The provisional criterion of adequacy C3 will take the form of a statement of identity conditions for languages. The reason is this: We are really asking, "What is the nature or essence of a language?" Now to ask, "What is the essence of an X?" is to ask, "What is it to be an X? In the case of a given X what is it to be *that* X? What is it to be identical with that X?" Thus the essence of a thing is tied up with its identity. (The foregoing is not quite Aristotle, but is psychologically quite close.) In the case of classes, for example, these questions are easily answered. Its membership is the essence of a class, its membership is what makes a class *that* class. For two classes are identical if they have the same membership and are different if they have different memberships. Any inquiry into the nature of entities of a certain category can most conveniently begin with a statement of the identity conditions for entities of that category.[1]

In the case of languages we have, as a first attempt:

C3. Two languages are identical if and only if (i) they have the same vocabulary and (ii) each expression of that common vocabulary has the same significance in one language as it has in the other.

Convention C3 is a criterion of adequacy in the sense that any definition of 'language', to be adequate, must logically imply C3. I have deliberately used the noncommittal word 'significance' in C3 rather than the word 'meaning'. For 'meaning' usually means 'intension', and although for *logical* signs *significance* coincides with *intension*, it will turn out that in regard to descriptive signs, if C3 used 'intension' rather than 'significance', we should have too stringent a set of identity conditions. But apart from the intended vagueness in the word 'significance' C3 would seem to have a certain *prima facie* suitability. However, the identity conditions stated in it make both the vocabulary and the assignment of significance *of the essence* of a language and on that account it will require some defence (by C2) in order to show that it has, not merely *prima facie*, but some degree of final suitability.

(i) *Vocabulary.* In his *Semantics*, p. 23, Carnap writes, "[In order to be able to write down actual examples of sentences of S_1, we may choose some letters as the first five signs, e.g. 'a', 'b', 'c', 'P', 'Q'. But this choice is obviously irrelevant for the semantical properties of S_1 and is therefore, strictly speaking, outside of pure semantics. Its role is the same as that of diagrams in geometry; they facilitate the operations practically but have no theoretical bearing on the proofs.]" This view has been propounded in some detail by Wilfrid Sellars (in *Identity, Quotes*) who regards a language as a set of linguistic roles. "One and the same language may have two or more sets of tokens. (Thus from the epistemological standpoint, English and German as

---

[1]But in some cases (e.g., that of properties) there may be no identity conditions. This point is urged in my *Property Designation*, §II.

empirically meaningful languages constitute two sets of token classes for the same type expressions.)"[2] Thus presumably English and German are merely two different embodiments of the same language. But at the level of common sense we should say that English and German are two different languages. An Englishman and a German, each familiar only with his mother tongue, would not succeed in intercommunicating. Thus the view is ruled out by C2. We shall, I think, be more likely to achieve clarity at the philosophical level if, on this point at least, we endorse common sense and regard the vocabulary of a language (its sets of unitary expressions or shapes or sign-designs) as of the essence of that language. What has happened in Carnap's *Semantics* is this: Carnap uses numerically subscripted Gothic symbols which are supposed to refer to the expressions of his object language. But since at no point does he *use* the object languages he can leave the Gothic symbols uninterpreted and assert, "Whatever I say is true under all interpretations of the Gothic symbols." In this way it is possible to maintain that although the vocabulary of a language is of its essence, semantics deals with languages at such a high level of generality that the semanticist need not specify the composition of the vocabulary of a language under study (and sometimes Carnap does not).

(ii) *Assignment of Significance.* From the fact that people use expressions and people use language we may be tempted to infer that a language *is* its vocabulary—a view at the other extreme from Sellars'. It is what I should call the fallacy of identifying language and vocabulary. It is a fallacy (assuming C2) for this reason: Suppose the Kwakiutl Indians used all and only the expressions of English but with different significations, so that when a Kwakiutl wishes to say, for example, that snow is white, he utters a token of 'Love is a many-splendoured thing'. Clearly an Englishman and a Kwakiutl would not succeed in exchanging information and from C2 we should infer that they use different languages. It is for this reason that it would seem wise to make the assignment of significance to the expressions of a language essential to that language.

But it should be noted that the convention does not make the *manner* in which a language is defined of its essence. In regard to other concepts this would be looked upon as a truism. We do not hold that '*x* is a three-sided plane figure' and '*x* is a three-angled plane figure' define different properties. Yet Carnap regards his S_1 and S_2 as different systems because of the different rules used in defining them. The system S_1 is a code system, S_2 is a language system. Yet they both have the

²Wilfrid Sellars, *RNWW*, p. 445 of the reprint in Feigl and Sellars, eds., *Readings.*

same expressions (which do not happen to be specified) and these expressions have the same significance in each language. On that account S_1 and S_2 would be regarded (by C3) as identical. Their differentiation is presumably a consequence of the doctrine already criticized that rules are constitutive of and not merely definitive of their languages.

Moreover the distinction between primitive sentence and theorem would not be of the essence of a language. I have already mentioned that we shall, to put it loosely, be constructing a language by first constructing an uninterpreted descriptive calculus and then supplying designation rules for the non-logical constants. If we take it that two calculi are logically equivalent if and only if every expression which is a sentence of one is a sentence of the other, and every sentence which is logically true (logically false, neither) in one is logically true (logically false, neither) in the other, and if a derivation relation holds in one it holds in the other, then on the present view (as defined by C3) equivalent calculi are in fact identical, because the logical signs of equivalent calculi have the same significance in both calculi. Thus to define a certain calculus, we might specify certain sentences as primitive sentences and certain sequences as direct derivations. But we could have defined the *same* calculus in alternative ways by specifying different primitive sentences and/or different direct derivations. Again the particular manner in which an entity (here a calculus) is defined is not essential to the entity defined. The identification of equivalent calculi is in accordance with the fact that in language as used it is not possible to draw any clear distinction between primitive sentence and theorem.

§7. A SECOND CRITERION OF ADEQUACY

Convention C3, however suitable in a general sort of way, is not sufficiently precise to work with. And so it may be expanded into:

C4. Two languages are identical if and only if (i) they have the same vocabulary, and (ii*a*) if an expression is designative in one language it is designative in the other and it G-designates the same entity in both languages, and (ii*b*) if an expression is a sentence of one language it is a sentence of the other, and if a sentence is logically true (logically false, neither) in one language then it is logically true (logically false, neither) in the other, and if E is a sentence of both languages and K a class of sentences of both languages then, if E is derivable from K in one language, E is derivable from K in the other.

Two key expressions occur in C4, 'logically true' and 'G-designates'. Thus we really have a package criterion of adequacy for all three of 'language', 'logically true' and 'G-designates'. As such it would be incomplete. I shall assume without explicit statement some such set of conventions for 'logically true' as occurs in Carnap's *Semantics*, p. 64. However, I shall use the term 'logically true' in a slightly novel sense. Although it is to be handled by methods more reminiscent of syntax than semantics, it does not mean 'provable'. Proofs occupy a curious status in the present method. They do not drop out altogether, as they do in orthodox semantics. However, a proof is always relative to a given method of specifying a language *L*. We specify the logically true sentences of a language by saying that such and such sentences (the primitive sentences) are logically true in *L* and also any sentence derivable from logically true sentences (that is, provable). The point of a proof is to convince us that, given the specification of the language, then the sentence *S* is a logically true sentence of the language. But given a different specification of the same language (that is, a listing of different primitive sentences) then that proof would not convince us and we should have to look for a different one. Thus a class of proofs is not of the essence of the language. The distinction between primitive sentence and theorem will recede into the background and it will take with it the concepts of *proof* and *provability*. On this account we may make the concept of logical truth broad enough to cover true Gödelian sentences.

The concept of G-designation, by reason of its apparent novelty, will require a fuller informal exposition. This will occupy us in the next two chapters.

III. THE METHOD, G

The concept of G-designation gets its character, not so much from a set of axioms governing the word 'G-designates', as from the total character of the metalanguage to be used. The simplest way of proceeding will be to present a sample language, which will be typical of the languages to be covered by our definition of 'language' and also of the non-semantical part of the metalanguage M. The general method to be used will be called 'G', to save us long-winded locutions like 'the present method'. The explanation and justification of the method will be postponed to a later section, for it is difficult to explain a method until it has been made clear precisely what it is that is to be explained. And so we shall begin with a little language, which we shall call 'L_2'. I shall be using a type of rule which has been shown in chapter I to be not altogether satisfactory, but it is a case of *faute de mieux*. For the most part, the phrase 'in L_2' will be omitted from the statement of the rules.

I. *Classification of signs*
   A. Primitive descriptive signs:
   Individual constants: 'a', 'b', 'c'.
   First order first degree predicate constants: 'P', 'P_1', 'P_2', 'Q'.
   First order second degree constants: 'R_1'.
   Second order first degree constants: 'ϕ_1', 'ψ_1'.

   B. Primitive logical signs:
   '$\supset$', '&', '$\vee$', '$\sim$', '$\exists$', '( )', '$=$'.
   Variables:
   Individual: 'x', 'y', 'z'.
   First order first degree: 'F', 'G'.
   First order second degree: 'R_1'.
   Second order first degree: 'ϕ_1'.
   Propositional: 'p', 'q'.

II. *Formation Rules*
   An expression E is a sentence of L_2 if and only if one of the following conditions is satisfied:

(a) E is of the form $E_1(E_j, E_k, \ldots, E_n)$, where $E_1, E_j, \ldots, E_n$ are descriptive constants or variables and E_1 is of the appropriate type (in which case E is an atomic sentence).

(b) E is of the form $E_1 = E_j$. Subject to the proviso that E_1 and E_j must be of the same type, each may be a primitive constant of any type, a predicate defined without the help of the identity sign, the connectives or quantifiers, or an atomic sentence, and one or both of E_1 and E_j may be a variable. (Identity sentences do not count as atomic sentences in G.)

(c) E is of the form $\smile E_j$ where E_j is a sentence, or is of the form $E_j \supset E_k$, or $E_j \& E_k$, or $E_j \lor E_k$, where E_j and E_k are both sentences.

(d) E is of the form $(v)(E_1)$ or of the form $(\exists v)(E_1)$ where E_1 is a sentence.

(e) E is the result of replacing a constant in a sentence by a Russellian definite description taking the smallest possible scope, or is the expansion of such a sentence.

III. *Transformation Rules*

A. All and only sentences of the following forms are axioms:[1]

1. $S_1 \supset (S_2 \supset S_1)$.
2. $[S_1 \supset (S_2 \supset S_3)] \supset [(S_1 \supset S_2) \supset (S_1 \supset S_3)]$.
3. $(S_1 \& S_2) \supset S_1$.
4. $(S_1 \& S_2) \supset S_2$.
5. $S_1 \supset [S_2 \supset (S_1 \& S_2)]$.
6. $S_1 \supset (S_1 \lor S_2)$.
7. $S_2 \supset (S_1 \lor S_2)$.
8. $(S_1 \supset S_3) \supset \{(S_2 \supset S_3) \supset [(S_1 \lor S_2) \supset S_3]\}$.
9. $(S_1 \supset S_2) \supset [(S_1 \supset \sim S_2) \supset \sim S_1]$.
10. $\sim\sim S_1 \supset S_1$.
11. $E_1 = E_1$.
12. $E_1 = E_2 \supset (S_1 \supset S_2)$ where S_1 contains E_1 and S_2 is the result of replacing E_1 in one, some, or all of its occurrences in S_1 by E_2, and if E_2 is a (Russellian) definite description then if E_1 is a definite description E_2 goes in with the same scope as E_1 has, and if E_1 is a constant E_2 goes in with the *smallest possible scope*. (This rule *permits* substitution with smallest possible scope where such substitution would not be justified by ordinary logic. It does not prohibit substitution with

---

[1]This axiom set is adapted from a set used by F. B. Fitch in teaching logic. (It is embedded in the system given in his *Intuitionistic.*) The changes here involve the addition of Axioms 11, 12, and 19. The advantage of the original system is that it permits fairly straightforward proof of the deduction theorem.

a larger scope where such substitution would be justified by ordinary logic. See §11.)

13. $(v)(S_1) \supset S_2$ where S_2 is the result of replacing all free occurrences of the variable v in S_1 by a constant or variable u provided that if u is a variable, no occurrences of v in S_1 are within the scope of a quantifier containing u as its variable.

14. $S_2 \supset (\exists v)(S_1)$ where (as in 13).

15. $(v)(S_1 \supset S_2) \supset [(v)(S_1) \supset (v)(S_2)]$.

16. $(v)(S_1 \supset S_2) \supset [(\exists v)(S_1) \supset (\exists v)(S_2)]$.

17. $S_1 \supset (v)(S_1)$

18. $(\exists v)(S_1) \supset S_1$ $\Big\}$ if v does not occur freely in S_1.

19. Identity conditions for (atomic) propositions:[2]

(a) $[E_{i1} = E_{j1} \ \& \ E_{i2} = E_{j2} \ \& \ \ldots \ \& \ E_{in} = E_{jn}] \supset$
$$E_{i1}(E_{i2}, \ldots, E_{in}) = E_{j1}(E_{j2}, \ldots, E_{jn}).$$

(b) $E_{i1}(E_{i2}, \ldots, E_{in}) = E_{j1}(E_{j2}, \ldots, E_{jn}) \supset [(E_{i1} = E_{j1} \ \& \ \ldots \ \&$
$E_{ik-1} = E_{jk-1} \ \& \ E_{ik+1} = E_{jk+1} \ \& \ \ldots \ \& \ E_{in} = E_{jn}) \supset$
$$E_{ik} = E_{jk}] \ (k = 1 \text{ to } n).$$

("Two propositions are identical if their corresponding constituents are identical. If two propositions are identical and all but one pair of corresponding constituents are identical then that pair of corresponding constituents are identical.")

20. $(v)(S_1)$ where S_1 is an axiom.

B. The Deduction Rule (Modus Ponens):

R1. S_3 is directly derivable from S_1 and S_2 if and only if the sequence $(S_1;S_2;S_3)$ is of the form:
$$S_1,$$
$$S_1 \supset S_3,$$
$$S_3.$$

IV. *Definitions*

LD1. The biconditional:
$$S_1 \equiv S_2 =_{df} (S_1 \supset S_2) \ \& \ (S_2 \supset S_1).$$

LD2. The iota operator:
$$-\{[(\imath x)(Fx)] \ldots (\imath x)(Fx) \ldots\} - =_{df}$$
$$-(\exists x)(Fy \equiv_y y = x \ \& \ldots x \ldots) -.$$

---

[2] This axiom is weaker—and for good reason—than the identity conditions laid down for propositions in *Property Designation*. Actually, Axiom 19(a) follows from Axiom 12, and moreover, it follows from Axiom 12 that if a description appears in the antecedent of 19(a) with small scope (as would normally be the case) then it appears in the consequent with small scope. Notwithstanding the derivability of 19(a) I am counting it as an axiom in order to have the (partial) identity conditions for propositions all in one place.

We may now define what it is to be a theorem of L_2:

MD1. E is a theorem of L_2 if and only if E is a member of every class K of sentences of L_2 which satisfies the following conditions: the axioms of L_2 are members of K and if E_i and E_j are members of K and E_k is directly derivable from E_i and E_j then E_k is a member of K.

What we have now is a descriptive calculus. Essentially it contains ordinary sentential and functional logic with a few added wrinkles involving the identity sign. We may convert it into a language by interpreting the non-logical signs, that is, by supplying G-designation rules for these constants:

> 'a'   G-designates New York (in L_2).
> 'b'   G-designates Chicago.
> 'c'   G-designates the sky.
> 'P'   G-designates Large.
> 'P_1' G-designates City.
> 'P_2' G-designates Windy.
> 'Q'   G-designates Blue.
> 'R_1' G-designates Larger Than.
> 'ϕ_1' G-designates Colour.
> 'ψ_1' G-designates Brilliant.

The sentence $E_i(E_j)$ G-designates the proposition that what E_j G-designates has the property that E_i G-designates (in L_2). The sentence E_i $(E_j, \ldots, E_n)$ G-designates the proposition that the relation G-designated by E_i obtains among the entities G-designates by $E_j, \ldots, E_n$ in that order.

Since 'G-designates' has been neither explained nor defined the rules will have to be read as: 'a' signifies New York, and so forth. It has already been mentioned that the language just outlined is intended as a model, both of the object languages to be covered subsequently by our definition of 'language' and also of the non-semantical parts of M. Generally, I shall use English as the metalanguage, but there will be places where we shall have to imagine the English translated into symbolic form. For example, an order of entities in the proposition that New York is larger than Chicago (i.e., the proposition $R_1(a,b)$) is: Larger Than, New York, Chicago.

Considered just in regard to its logical character, L_2 has a few novel and perhaps unprepossessing features, and these had best be brought into the full light of day at once. In the first place we recognize primitive properties and properties defined without the help of logical signs other than variables.[3] And since we recognize properties we shall want to be able to say things like 'This property is identical with that property' and 'This property is distinct from that property even though they are co-extensive' ('$P \neq Q \ \& \ P \equiv Q$'). Obviously L_2 is non-extensional if by an extensional language we mean a language in which co-extensive expressions are everywhere interchangeable. (It will transpire that L_2 is also non-intensional.) Since we do *not* recognize properties defined with the help of logical signs other than variables, we shall not permit the corresponding predicates to appear as arguments of identity sentences *nor to serve as value expressions of variables*. That is, we shall not countenance the following kind of argument: since New York is large or blue, and the sky is large or blue, there exists a property which both New York and the sky have in common. Symbolically:

$$\text{Let } P_3x =_{df} Px \lor Qx$$
$$\left.\begin{array}{l} Pa \\ Qc \end{array}\right\} \text{Premises}$$
$$\therefore Pa \lor Qa$$
$$\text{and } \ Pc \lor Qc$$
$$\therefore \ P_3a$$
$$\text{and } \ P_3c \qquad\qquad \text{Df.}$$
$$\therefore P_3a \ \& \ P_3c$$
$$\therefore (\exists F)(Fa \ \& \ Fc).$$

Furthermore, we recognize atomic propositions. And doing so, we shall want to be able to say that this proposition is identical with (or distinct from) that proposition. That is why we shall use the identity sign between atomic sentences and permit atomic sentences to be replaced by quantifiable propositional variables. But we do not recognize identity or molecular or general propositions, and on that account we do not permit identity sentences, molecular sentences, or general sentences to appear in argument places (either *in* identity sentences or on the right-hand side of designation statements) or to be replaced by propositional variables—except as allowed by Formation Rule (*e*).

All that has been said so far holds for both the object languages and for the non-semantical part of *M*. But in *M* we shall have G-

[3]For years properties have been under attack by Quine. In the papers *Property Designation* and *Space* I have, among other things, tried to defend properties against Quine's specific strictures.

designation statements which have no counterpart in the object languages. Without apology or explanation I shall simply lay down two axioms governing such statements. The first is a univocity requirement.

GAx1. If E G-designates e_i in L and E G-designates e_j in L then $e_i = e_j$.

A consequence of GAx1 is that if, in a certain language, an expression G-designates Human then it does *not* G-designate Featherless-bipedal. For even though Human is co-extensive with Featherless-bipedal, it is not identical with it. Thus 'G-designates' is a non-extensional relation word.

The second axiom stipulates that only names (or, designators), not descriptions, are in the field of the relation of G-designation.

GAx2. If E is a definite description, or is an expression containing a definite description, or is defined with the help of a definite description, then E does not G-designate anything.

It remains in the next section to generalize the notion of a definite description.

§9. DESCRIPTIONS OF ENTITIES OTHER THAN INDIVIDUALS

The reason for recognizing properties is both simple and decisive. In order to say what 'b' signifies we have to mention the city of Chicago. Likewise, in order to say what 'Q' signifies we have to mention the property, Blue. That is, we have to say, " 'Q' signifies Blue," in which 'Blue' appears in an argument place and is therefore replaceable by a bound variable. (It will have to be shown subsequently that the class of blue things will not serve the purpose. See below, p. 45.) It might be suggested that we could explain the significance of 'Q' by saying that a full sentence of 'Q' with an individual constant is *true* if and only if the individual signified by that constant is blue— *if we already had a definition of 'true'.* But we do not in the beginning have such a definition.

Since we are recognizing properties (e.g., Blue) we should be able to refer to properties by definite descriptions (e.g., 'the colour of the sky'). As a matter of fact it ought to be possible to refer to any entity by description. At any rate we lay down the following definition of property descriptions in analogy to Russell's definition of individual descriptions. For simplicity the scope symbol is omitted.

LD3. $—(\imath F)(\ldots F \ldots)—\ =_{\text{df}}\ (\exists F)[(\ldots G \ldots)\ \equiv_{\text{G}}\ G\ =\ F\ \&\ —F—].$

For example, the sentences, 'a is (has) the colour of c' and 'the colour of c is brilliant' would be written '$[(\imath F)(\phi_1 F\ \&\ Fc)]a$' and '$\psi_1[(\imath F)(\phi_1 F\ \&\ Fc)]$' and expanded respectively as:

$$(\exists F)[(\phi_1 G\ \&\ Gc)\ \equiv_{\text{G}}\ G\ =\ F\ \&\ Fa],$$
$$(\exists F)[(\phi_1 G\ \&\ Gc)\ \equiv_{\text{G}}\ G\ =\ F\ \&\ \psi_1 F].$$

Now descriptions, unlike names, do not G-designate entities. But if a description is fulfilled (i.e., has a descriptum) then we may say that it *refers* to the descriptum. (That is, 'the author of *Waverley*' does not G-designate, but does refer to, Walter Scott.) We shall say in general that a description is referential whether it has a descriptum or not. Names, of course, also refer to the entities they G-designate. If two expressions E_i and E_j, whether names or descriptions, refer to the same entity we shall say that they are *co-referential*. In such a case, and only in such a case, the identity sentence with E_i and E_j as arguments will be true. The consequence of Axiom 12 and R1 jointly may be expressed metalinguistically as follows:

Two co-referential expressions are everywhere interchangeable, and if a description is substituted for a name it takes the smallest possible scope.

This procedure represents a very strong interpretation of the identity sign and it will require a full discussion subsequently. For the moment we shall concentrate on consequences. But before leaving the matter of property descriptions, it would be well to mention that we shall find a second type of property description, which results from the interchangeability rule and the recognition of atomic propositions.

If we are going to recognize propositions, then we ought to be able to refer to them by description, as for example, 'the first proposition of Caesar's *De Bello Gallico*' might be a description of the proposition that all Gaul is divided into three parts. Actually, this type of proposition description plays no part in subsequent discussion. But another type of proposition description emerges by reason of the interchangeability rule. Consider the following argument:

Chicago is large = Chicago is large.
Chicago = the windy city.
Chicago is large = the windy city is large.

Symbolically, the argument would be as follows:

(1) $Pb = Pb.$
(2) $b = (\imath x)(P_1x \And P_2x).$
(3) $\therefore Pb = [(\imath x)(P_1x \And P_2x)]P(\imath x)(P_1x \And P_2x).$

Statement (3) follows by Ax.12 and R1 from (1) and (2). If Ax.19(*a*) carried a rider to the effect that descriptions take small scope with them, then it would follow directly by Ax.19(*a*) and R1.

Now in virtue of the identity of the proposition that Chicago is large and the proposition that the windy city is large, we simply do not have two distinct propositions to serve as G-designata of the sentences, 'Chicago is large' and 'the windy city is large'. The sentences are co-referential, to be sure ((3) being true), and so we take the view that the latter is a *description* of the proposition that Chicago is large, and as such does not G-designate anything. By 'singular sentence' let us understand 'a sentence which is either atomic or is the result of replacing a constant in an atomic sentence by a description'. Now we take the more general view that any singular sentence containing a description is a description of, but does not G-designate, a proposition. Sentences containing descriptions expand into multiply general sentences and so we take the further step of deciding that *no* general or molecular sentence is designative, and unless it contracts to a singular sentence it will not even be referential.

We are, in fact, refusing to recognize identity or molecular or general propositions. This decision is already embodied in Formation Rule (*b*), where it is laid down that atomic sentences, but not identity or molecular or general sentences (except as allowed by Formation Rule (*e*)) may appear in argument places. The decision to exclude identity, molecular, and general sentences from the class of designative expressions and—what is not quite the same thing in view of a class of non-designative referential expressions—the decision to exclude such sentences from argument places unless they are contractible to singular sentences, is, as far as I know, not forced at this point. But it will save us a host of complications in chapter v. The reasons for *retaining* atomic propositions will become fully apparent only in chapter vi.

One small point before proceeding. We shall have a rule,

(4) '*Pb*' G-designates in L_2 (the proposition that) Chicago is large,

from which may be derived, on the basis either of (3) or of (2) and the rules,

(5)   '*Pb*' G-designates in L_2 (the proposition that) [scope symbol] the
       windy city is large.

It may seem odd, but it is actually unobjectionable that 'the windy
city is large' may appear on the right-hand side (RHS) of G-designation statements but that " 'the windy city is large' " may *not* appear
on the LHS—not to make a true G-designation statement, that is.
(Descriptions, it will be recalled, do not G-designate.) Statement (5)
can be taken to mean that '*Pb*' G-designates what the last five words
of (5) describe. It is not a rule of language (as is (4)), but simply a
factual truth depending on the truth of (2). Statement (5) is in much
the same case as the factually true sentences,

(6)   '*b*' G-designates the windy city,
(7)   '*Q*' G-designates the colour of the sky.

These follow respectively from the rules and the factual truths,
'Chicago = the windy city' and 'Blue = the colour of the sky'.

§10. INTENSIONAL PROPOSITIONS AND G-PROPOSITIONS

Now let us pause for a while. There are two things which perhaps
puzzle the reader. One is the placing of the scope symbol in (3), and
the other is the apparently carefree way in which substitutions are
made without regard to the character of the context. I shall deal
with the second matter first.

It will be urged that propositions are intensions and that propositional identity must be defined in terms of necessary equivalence:

(8) $p = q \equiv N(p \equiv q)$.

Thus a statement of propositional identity such as (1) is not a
context in which expressions which are co-extensive but not co-
intensional ('Chicago' and 'the windy city') are interchangeable. The
same uneasy feeling may be aroused over the present treatment of
properties. Properties are the intensions of predicates (it will be said)
and property identity will turn on necessary equivalence of matrices.
Yet we are holding that Blue is identical with the colour of the sky
and would presumably go on to assert that the property of being
blue is identical with the property of being the colour of the sky,
despite the lack of logical equivalence between the expressions in
question.

A simple way of characterizing the method G is as follows. We adopt a strict interpretation of identity (which has yet to be justified): whatever you say about one of two identical entities you may say about the other. Next we take up the two well-known empirical facts that Chicago is identical with the windy city and that blue is identical with the colour of the sky. Now we merely look around for a method which will not compel us in effect to deny these facts by forcing us to place restrictions on the interchange of co-referential expressions. We stick to the rule of interchange and simply do not worry about contexts. It is true that the language is non-intensional (as well as being non-extensional), if by an intensional language we understand a language in which only co-intensional expressions are everywhere interchangeable. And it is true that our propositions and properties are not intensions. It might be suggested that all we have succeeded in doing is fabricating new and strange entities that scarcely deserve the appellations 'property' and 'proposition'. It would be replied that, after all, the properties and propositions of G are what the predicate and propositional variables of G range over. It will be convenient subsequently to speak of G-properties and G-propositions where it is necessary to contrast them with the more familiar intensional properties and propositions. For the most part, however, the prefix will be omitted.

I might at this point make two further observations. The first concerns (8), the statement of identity conditions for intensional propositions. Logical equivalence of expressions should *never* be made the condition of identity for entities of a certain kind. For as soon as you recognize an entity you can always find a way of referring to it by a description which is *not* logically equivalent to its name. For example, 'the first proposition of Caesar's *De Bello Gallico*' is not logically equivalent to 'the proposition that all Gaul is divided into three parts'. (This point seems to me to be both decisive and important.)

And in the second place I think I should deny that there is anything so very novel about G-propositions. There are actually two distinct traditions regarding the "nature" of propositions. According to the first (Frege, Carnap's *M & N*) a proposition is the intension of a sentence, and statement (8) would presumably express the identity conditions for propositions. As an intension, a proposition contains, not individuals, but individual concepts, which are the *intensions* of individual constants. According to the second and more subterranean tradition, a proposition is constituted out of one or more individuals and a property or relation of appropriate degree. The identity conditions for propositions would be expressed by Axiom 19. Thus from the standpoint of the intension-extension distinction, propositions of this second sort are hybrids. The method G is an elaboration of this second tradition. As such it is simplicity itself: we recognize the individual Chicago, the property Large, and the proposition that Chicago is large, which is composed of the individual Chicago and the property Large. And we do our best to forget about the intension-extension distinction.

Signs of the second tradition are to be found in the early parts of Carnap's *Semantics* (where return of the intension-extension distinction produces a certain amount of incoherence).[4] Signs of it are also scattered throughout Russell's writings, where Russell speaks of the constituents of propositions, and it is clear he means that individuals rather than individual concepts constitute propositions. Oddly enough, if we take the second tradition seriously, we have to conclude that Russell was wrong in denying that the author of *Waverley* (i.e., Scott) is a constituent of the proposition that the author of *Waverley* (i.e., Scott) is Scotch. What Russell was rightly concerned to maintain is that the sentence, 'The author of *Waverley* is Scotch', does not gain its significance by referring to the proposition that the author of *Waverley* is Scotch. It would have what significance it has even if there were no proposition that the author of *Waverley* is Scotch—as would be the case if there were no such individual as *the* author of *Waverley*. (A description does not have significance by referring to an individual. It has significance, or better, is significant, by being composed in a significant way of expressions which in one way or another are significant in their own right.)

§11. NARROW SCOPES FOR DESCRIPTIONS[5]

We may now return to the first matter which may have bothered the reader, namely, the placing of the scope symbol of the description in the conclusion of argument (1)–(3). If we expand statement (2) *à la* Russell (i.e., LD2 of §8) and apply ordinary rules of logic we should be able to infer, not

$$(3) \quad Pb = [(\imath x)(P_1 x \ \& \ P_2 x)] P(\imath x)(P_1 x \ \& \ P_2 x)$$

[4] See Church, *Rev. Carnap.*

[5] In what follows I am indebted to some penetrating criticisms of my *Property Designation*, communicated to me privately by A. F. Smullyan.

which expands into

(9) $Pb = (\exists x)[(P_1y \,\&\, P_2y) \equiv_y y = x \,\&\, Px]$

but rather,

(10) $(\exists x)[(P_1y \,\&\, P_2y) \equiv_y y = x \,\&\, Px = Pb]$

which contracts into

(11) $[(\imath x)(P_1x \,\&\, P_2x)]Pb = P(\imath x)(P_1x \,\&\, P_2x)$

in which the description has the larger of the two possible scopes. It is clear that in substituting with small scope (as in (3)) we are using an "original" rule of interchange, that is, one not derivable from elementary logic, and this rule must be built into the axiom set in the form of a special stipulation. Such a stipulation has been added to Axiom 12 and so argument (1)–(3) is unquestionably valid according to our rules. There is now the question as to the reason for this stipulation.

If we had modal operators and statement (8) as a statement of identity conditions for propositions, then (3) would be provably false. But suppose we had neither modal operators *nor* the original rule of interchange. What should we then do with (3)? I think we have to regard it as meaningful. (Hence Formation Rule (*e*).) For (10) and (11) are both meaningful, since they are derived by conventional means from (1) and (2), which are both meaningful. And surely we may take it that if a sentence is meaningful with the scope symbol occurring in one appropriate place then it is meaningful with the scope symbol occurring in another appropriate place. And the scope symbol of (3) occurs "appropriately" in the sense that if everything preceding it is dropped then the remainder is meaningful by ordinary standards, even though the scope symbol would now be superfluous.

And so (3) is meaningful but neither provable nor refutable. It must therefore be factually true or false. But it cannot be true simply by reason of the fact that Chicago is identical with the windy city, for in that case (3) would be derivable from (2), which *ex hypothesi* it is not. In short (3) has no truth conditions and our system suffers from a kind of incompleteness. To complete it we should have to add either modal operators and statement (8) as an axiom, or the stipulation of Axiom 12 regarding the choice of narrow scopes for descriptions. The argument now becomes one as to the relative merits of intensional propositions and G-propositions, and my final remarks will have to wait until chapter VI. But if it can be assumed that we do not want to be bothered with modal operators, then enough has been said already to justify the original rule of interchange. Moreover, with the strong interchangeability rule we are able to retain Russell's rule which states that if a description is fulfilled, the scope symbol may be shuffled about *salva veritate*.

§12. SOME RESULTS

In what follows nothing very new will emerge, but in §8 certain decisions were more or less forced by prior decisions and here we shall be concerned simply to see how they were forced.

(*a*) *Propositions may be identical even though no component of one is identical with the corresponding component of the other.* For example, let us define 'is smaller than':

$$S(x,y) =_{df} R_1(y,x).$$
$$\text{Now } R_1(a,b) = R_1(a,\, b)$$
$$\therefore\ R_1(a,b) = S(b,a) \qquad\qquad \text{Df.}$$

Thus we have two propositions identical without term by term identity. It is for this reason that Axiom 19(*a*) has to be given as a conditional, not as a biconditional, and supplemented with Axiom 19(*b*).

(*b*) *A sentence may be non-designative even if it is logically equivalent to a designative sentence.* Consider the sentence:

(12) $Pa = [Pa\ \&\ (Qc \lor \sim\!Qc)].$

There is no way of proving this sentence in a non-modal language. Therefore we shall not wish to call it true. And for similar reasons we shall not wish to call it false. We have no alternative but to declare that it is meaningless and that its RHS is non-designative. The matter has already been taken care of by the earlier stipulation that molecular sentences are non-designative. And we have no reason for wishing to make an exception of those molecular sentences which happen to be logically equivalent to atomic sentences. Nevertheless it might seem surprising that '$Pa\ \&\ (Qc \lor \sim\!Qc)$', although logically equivalent to 'Pa', does not G-designate whatever proposition 'Pa' G-designates. The reason, of course, is that G-propositions are not intensions and L-equivalence is not a necessary condition of sentential co-reference, and (what has just come out) is not even a sufficient condition of sentential co-reference. The sentence 'Pa' gets its significance simply from G-designating the proposition that New York is large. But '$Pa\ \&\ (Qc \lor$

$\sim Qc)'$ has a more complicated kind of significance commensurate with its more complicated structure. It is also worth noting the reason why (12) is not provable. It is because a statement of propositional identity is neither molecular nor general nor genuinely atomic. At any rate the argument sentences are not components in the same way in which they might be components of a molecular or general sentence. On this account they are not accessible to manipulation by ordinary sentential and functional logic. That is, we cannot take '$Pa = Pa$', extract one side, manipulate it to get 'Pa & $(Qc \lor \sim Qc)$' and replace the result in the original identity statement. We should not want to regard 'A' and 'B' as interchangeable in an identity statement simply on the strength of the truth of '$A \equiv B$'. It might be that '$A \equiv B$' is provable, but we cannot make this fact relevant without modal operators. And so we see that sentences *in* identity sentences suffer from a sort of *logical isolation*. The same is true of a sentence in any argument place, for example, on the RHS of a G-designation statement.

(*c*) *If there are no identity or molecular or general propositions then there are no complex defined properties, and conversely.* By 'a complex defined property' we mean a property whose definition uses the identity sign, connectives or quantifiers. Example:

$$Q_1 x =_{df} P_1 x \lor P_2 x.$$

We are assuming that there are no molecular or general propositions, that is, that molecular and general sentences may not appear as arguments of identity sentences. Now let us suppose that there is the molecular property Q_1 (i.e., that 'Q_1' is designative and may appear in argument places). We have:

$$
\begin{array}{rcll}
Q_1 & = & Q_1 & \\
b & = & b & \\
\therefore \quad Q_1 b & = & Q_1 b & \text{Ax. 19}(a) \\
\therefore P_1 b \lor P_2 b & = & P_1 b \lor P_2 b & \text{Df.}
\end{array}
$$

Now we have a molecular sentence as an argument of an identity sentence, contrary to our initial assumption. Hence the supposition that 'Q_1' can be designative must be false. Similarly for any other complex defined property. The converse part of the theorem raises a type of question which will be dealt with in (*d*).

(*d*) *If there are atomic propositions there are simple defined properties.* By 'a simple defined property' we mean a property whose definition does not contain the identity sign, connectives or quantifiers. Example:

$$Q_2x =_{df} R_1(x,a).$$

Now $R_1 = R_1$ & $b = b$ & $a = a$

∴	$R_1(b,a) = R_1(b,a)$	Ax. 19(a)
∴	$Q_2b = Q_2b$	Df.
∴	$Q_2 = Q_2$	Ax. 19(b).

We are concluding that since the deduction procedures yield an expression containing 'Q_2' in an argument place, 'Q_2' is designative and there is the property Q_2. Strictly speaking, the argument is inconsequent, because the eligibility of an expression to appear as the conclusion of a proof presupposes that it is a sentence, and that is precisely what is in question in the case of '$Q_2 = Q_2$'. The same *non sequitur* would appear in the attempt to prove the converse in (c). At most, what has been shown here is that recognition of simple defined properties is in harmony with our other decisions. In the final analysis it rests on an intuition that if it is possible to combine Larger Than, New York, and Chicago to form the proposition that New York is larger than Chicago, then it ought to be possible to combine Larger Than and Chicago to form the property of being larger than Chicago. We could abandon simple defined properties without impairing the effectiveness of G, and I now suspect that there might be certain advantages in doing so.

(e) *Simple defined descriptional predicates are never designative but are referential.* By a 'simple defined descriptional predicate' we mean a predicate whose definition contains a description, but not the identity sign, connectives or quantifiers. The term 'referential' means 'refers to something or at least purports to do so'. An example of a simple defined descriptional predicate would be 'Q_3', defined as follows:

$$Q_3x =_{df} R_1(x,(\imath y)(Qy)).$$

Now suppose that as a matter of fact the description '$(\imath y)(Qy)$' has no descriptum, that is,

	$\sim[(\imath y)(Qy)](\imath y)(Qy) = (\imath y)(Qy)$	
∴	$R_1(b,(\imath y)(Qy)) \neq R_1(b,(\imath y)(Qy))$	Ax. 19(b)
∴	$Q_3b \neq Q_3b$	Df.
But	$b = b$	
∴	$Q_3 \neq Q_3$	Ax. 19(a).

Thus, given our supposition, 'Q_3' refers to no property, and *a fortiori* does not G-designate a property. The conclusion is in much the same case as 'The king of France in 1905 $\neq$ the king of France in 1905'.

Again, suppose, contrary to the above, that

$$(\imath y)(Qy) = a.$$

Now	$b = b \ \& R_1 = R_1$	
$\therefore$	$R_1(b,a) = R_1(b,(\imath y)(Qy))$	Ax. 19(a).
But	$R_1(b,a) = Q_2 b$	Df.
And	$R_1(b,(\imath y)(Qy)) = Q_3 b$	Df.
$\therefore$	$Q_2 b = Q_3 b$	Trans. of Id.
$\therefore$	$Q_2 = Q_3$	Ax. 19(b).

Thus, given our second supposition, Q_3 is a description of —refers to— the property designated by 'Q_2'. These simple defined descriptional predicates are the second kind of property description alluded to in §9.

The foregoing is intended to take care of a situation that puzzles Quine in Part V of his *Notes*. He observes that with ordinary interchange the following argument would be valid:

(13)   the attribute of exceeding 9 = the attribute of exceeding 9,
(14)   the number of planets = 9,
(15)   the attribute of exceeding the number of planets = the
          attribute of exceeding 9.

Quine is puzzled because the premises are true and the conclusion, offhand, would seem to be false. With the present method, the conclusion is true, the LHS of (15) being a property description referring to the property G-designated by the RHS.[6]

§13. THE UNRESTRICTED RULE OF INTERCHANGE

We are placing a very strong interpretation on the sign of identity. That is, we are using a strong interchangeability rule: co-referential expressions are interchangeable in all contexts; whatever you say about one of two identical entities you may say about the other. My own feeling is that if identity does not mean universal interchangeability then I do not really understand identity at all. Apart from our intuitions in the matter there are certain systematic considerations in favour of the present interpretation of identity. Assuming that we are unwilling to tolerate the kind of incompleteness mentioned in connec-

---

[6]A fuller treatment of the whole matter of property description and of Quine's problem is to be found in *Property Designation*. It should be stated also that the present approach owes a very great deal to the stimulus of Quine's papers, and particularly Part v of his *Notes*.

tion with the question of scopes for descriptions, then we are confronted with a choice between G and modal logic. Any argument against modal logic is an argument for the method G and its strict interpretation of identity. However, the rule of interchange gives rise to some well-known contradictions. It is apparently possible to derive false statements from true ones. I shall simply give examples of the kinds of derivations and indicate how we should deal with them. The modalities come up for discussion in (*d*).

(a) Quotation contexts

$$\text{Tully} = \text{Cicero}$$
'Cicero' has six letters
∴ 'Tully' has six letters.

We avoid this result by stipulating that quoted contexts are not contexts accessible to interchange, or rather that they are not contexts at all. (We thus justify the use of the phrase 'all contexts' in the statement of the rule of interchange.) As Quine has pointed out, 'Cicero' does not occur in " 'Cicero' " any more than 'cat' occurs in 'cattle'.

(b)   Property (attribute) expressions

The example here involves the identity of the number of planets with the number 9 and has been dealt with at the end of §12.

(c) Intentional contexts

Walter Scott = the author of *Waverley*

George IV wondered if Walter Scott is identical with the author of *Waverley*

∴ George IV wondered if Walter Scott is identical with Walter Scott.

I do not believe that we are yet ready to handle the intentional contexts, statements of assertion, belief, etc. Suffice it to say that these statements will not be admitted into the languages of G. This is a legitimate gambit since it is reasonable to suppose that we shall be able eventually to supply unobjectionable metalinguistic resources for saying substantially what is conveyed by ordinary statements of belief and assertion. I should conjecture that with a few alterations, Carnap's method of intensional isomorphism would serve.[7]

---

[7]See *M & N*, §§13, 14. And see below, p. 123 for an emendation to Church's emendation.

(d) *Modal Contexts*

Walter Scott = the author of *Waverley*
Necessarily (Walter Scott = Walter Scott)
∴ Necessarily (Walter Scott = the author of *Waverley*).

The conclusion is false. The fact that 'Walter Scott' and 'the author of *Waverley*' are not interchangeable *salva veritate* in 'Necessarily (Walter Scott = Walter Scott)' leads Quine to conclude that (in a modal language) Walter Scott is *not* identical with the author of *Waverley*. Thus in a modal language the individual variables range over individual concepts—intensions—rather than individuals. (More accurately, the individuals of a modal language are individual concepts rather than ordinary concrete individuals.) The paradox here leads Quine to take a very dim view of modal logic. His attacks on modal logic (in *Notes*, *Modal Logic*, *Rev. Barcan*, and Carnap's *M & N*, pp. 196–7) focus essentially on the point that modal languages do not accommodate the unrestricted rule of interchange. Thus his arguments are arguments *for* such an interchangeability rule. If they are cogent, then they apply against the admission of *any* contexts requiring restrictions on interchange.

Some modal systems recognize two kinds of identity, necessary and contingent. Commenting on one of these systems, Quine writes (*Rev. Barcan*, p. 96), "As is to be expected only the strong kind of identity is subject to a law of substitutivity valid for all modal contexts. It should be noted that only the strong kind of identity is therefore interpretable as identity in the ordinary sense of the word." I take it that Quine is really asking if it makes sense to talk about two kinds of (numerical) identity. If two individuals are (numerically) identical, they are identical, and that is the end of the matter. That is, if two objects are really one, that is all there is to it. It does not make sense to say that in a weak sense they are one and in a strong sense two. If there are two species of identity then there ought to be a generic concept, just as for the two species of truth, logical and factual, there is a generic concept of truth. But there is no such generic concept of identity. We might take it that after all, interchangeability is the linguistic correlate of identity and we can distinguish two species of interchangeability: interchangeability in all contexts and interchangeability in all and only non-modal contexts. But this will not do because the linguistic correlate of numerical identity is not just interchangeability, but rather *universal* interchangeability. (And while we are on the subject, qualitative identity and numerical identity are not two species of a generic identity, for the former is definable in terms of the latter. If by 'qualitative identity' we mean the possession of all non-spatial properties in common, then two objects are qualitatively identical if and only if every non-spatial property of one is *numerically* identical with some non-spatial property of the other.)

At any rate, Quine construes the antinomy, not as an objection to the interchangeability rule, but as an objection to modal logic, and it seems to me that he is right. A variety of considerations—both the present one and others—lead us to exclude modal operators from G. With this manœuvre, the antinomies to which the rule of interchange gives rise in modal logic no longer embarrass us. There is one alternative open to us: We can assimilate modal contexts to quotation contexts. And since quotation contexts are not really contexts at all, failure of interchange would cause us no psychological discomfort or systematic inconvenience.[8]

A. F. Smullyan (in *Modalities*) suggests an interesting way in which one might attempt to deal with the last mentioned antinomy. Let us rewrite the argument symbolically:

$$s = (\imath x)(Wx)$$
$$N(s = s)$$
$$N(s = (\imath x)(Wx)).$$

Assuming that we are using Russellian descriptions, where are we to place the scope symbol in the conclusion so as to resolve its ambiguity? If we take small scope we get the false sentence,

$$N\{[(\imath x)(Wx)]s = (\imath x)(Wx)\}$$

or:

$$N[(\exists x)(Wy \equiv_y y = x \ \& \ s = x)].$$

But Smullyan is concerned to point out that if we expand the first premise according to Russell's contextual definition of descriptions and use ordinary deduction we get the *true* statement,

$$(\exists x)[Wy \equiv_y y = x \ \& \ N(s = x)]$$

or,

$$[(\imath x)(Wx)]N\{s = (\imath x)(Wx)\}.$$

Smullyan would say that all the antinomy shows is that a certain amount of care has to be taken in placing the scope symbol in sentences containing both modal and iota operators. We place the scope symbol where ordinary deduction will permit us to place it. Thus we have a system containing modal operators whose individual variables seem to range over ordinary individuals instead of individual concepts.

[8]This suggestion is made in greater detail in *Property Designation*. pp. 392–3.

It might be replied that this technique works nicely where one of the co-referential expressions is a description and one can exercise a certain amount of judicious control over the placing of the scope symbol. But what about the following?

$$\text{Tully} = \text{Cicero}$$
$$\text{Necessarily (Cicero} = \text{Cicero})$$
$$\therefore \text{Necessarily (Tully} = \text{Cicero})$$

It could be maintained that although the premises are true the conclusion is false. My own feeling is that the sentence, 'Tully = Cicero' is so enshrouded in mystery that we are not in a very good position to know whether it is necessarily or contingently true, and that as a consequence we can make no decisive polemical use of it.

But suppose we let '$(\imath x)(Mx)$' mean 'the author of *Marmion*' and 'S' mean 'Scotch'. Now consider the argument,

$$(\imath x)(Wx) = (\imath x)(Mx)$$
$$\text{N}\{[(\imath x)(Wx)]S(\imath x)(Wx) \equiv [(\imath x)(Wx)]S(\imath x)(Wx)\}$$
$$\therefore \text{N}\{[(\imath x)(Wx)]S(\imath x)(Wx) \equiv [(\imath x)(Mx)]S(\imath x)(Mx)\}.$$

The premises are true and the conclusion, obtained by substitution, is false. What *could* be obtained by deduction is:

$$[(\imath x)(Wx)][(\imath x)(Mx)]\text{N}\{S(\imath x)(Wx) \equiv S(\imath x)(Mx)\}.$$

Here it is not a question of substituting a description for a name and then judiciously choosing the scope. If we wish to substitute '$(\imath x)(Mx)$' on the RHS of '$\equiv$' in the second premise, the scope is already selected. Thus we are forced to conclude that '$(\imath x)(Wx)$' and '$(\imath x)(Mx)$' are not interchangeable in all modal contexts and that within a modal language the author of *Waverley* is not identical with the author of *Marmion*. Since identity is a transitive relation we dare not say that nevertheless they are both identical with Walter Scott. In general then, the individuals of a modal language are individual concepts rather than ordinary concrete individuals.

A defender of the modalities might reply, "So what? It is true that in a modal language the individual variables do not range over the same entities as the individual variables of a non-modal language range over. And it is true that in a modal language the sign '$=$' as occurring in '$(\imath x)(Wx) = (\imath x)(Mx)$' is not a proper sign of identity in the traditional sense. But everything you may wish to say in a non-modal language can be said in a modal language, and a great deal more besides. What are you complaining about?"

I do not think that at this point any really decisive complaints against the modalities can be made. But I think it is apparent that modal languages are so paradoxical that if a procedure ignores modal operators altogether then it does not have to apologize for doing so. And in §14 we may find that for our purposes there is a decisive objection to modal languages, because in a modal language it is possible to mention intensions but not extensions.

§14. G-DESIGNATION AND THE CRITERIA OF ADEQUACY

Many of the features of G have already been given some kind of justification in terms of prior decisions. What now has to be undertaken is the justification of the method as a whole. In particular, we shall have to show that C4 is a "suitable" elaboration of C3 with and only with 'G-designates'.

Let us use the expression 'E-designates' for the extensional designation relation used in Carnap's *Semantics*. Now if, in C4, 'G-designates' were replaced by 'E-designates' we should not have a suitable elaboration of C3. For suppose we have two languages that differ only in that in one 'Scott' has the same significance as the English phrase 'the author of *Waverley*' and in the other it has the same significance as the English name 'Walter Scott'. Thus the expression 'Scott' would have the same E-designatum in both languages and by C4-with-'E-designates', the languages would be identical. But on our admittedly vague understanding of 'significance' I think we should judge that 'Scott' has a different significance in each of the languages and that the languages are therefore different. Thus C4-with-'E-designates' would not be a suitable elaboration of C3.

The following consideration is perhaps more decisive. Suppose we have a language in which '*H*' has the same significance as the English word 'human'. Thus in the language '*H*' E-designates Human. Let us assume for the sake of the example that there is a property Featherless-bipedal and that it is co-extensive with the property Human. Since 'E-designates' is extensional we shall also have it that '*H*' E-designates Featherless-bipedal. Thus the predicate '*H*' has at least two designata, Human and Featherless-bipedal. (Alternatively, and especially if the metalanguage is completely extensional, we may say that it has only *one* designatum, namely, the *class* of humans, which is identical with the class of featherless bipeds, but the following difficulty arises in any case.) And suppose we have a second language exactly like the first except that in it '*H*' has the same significance as the English phrase 'featherless biped'. Again '*H*' E-designates both Human and Featherless-bipedal, or alternatively, the class. By our informal understanding of 'significance' we should judge that '*H*' has a different significance in the two languages and that (by C3) the two languages are therefore distinct. But by C4-with-'E-designates', they would be regarded as the same. Again, therefore, E-designation will not serve our purpose because it does not yield a suitable elaboration of C3. Obviously, the considerations involved also militate against basing semantics on classes rather than properties.

If it were said that the languages would differ in that in one '*H*' E-designates Human in virtue of a rule and Featherless-bipedal in virtue of fact, and in the other language vice versa, I should agree. *But in a non-intensional (i.e., non-modal) metalanguage we cannot record this difference.*

And so let us follow Carnap from his *Semantics* to his *M & N* and try to exploit the concept of intension. We offer the following as an elaboration of C3:

C4'. Two languages are identical if and only if they have the same vocabulary and each expression of that vocabulary has the same intension in one language as it has in the other.

Carnap tells us (*M & N*, p. 112) that "the semantical rule for a sign has to state primarily its intension; the extension is secondary. . . ." Now if you ask, "What is the intension of 'blue'?" I can tell you: Blue. But how is one to answer the question, "What is the intension of 'Scott'?" If you say, "Walter Scott," you are wrong, because Walter Scott is not the intension of 'Scott', he is the *extension*. The question, "What is the extension of 'Scott'?" can be answered by saying, "The extension is Walter Scott." Since we have no means of saying what the intension of an individual constant is, the method of intension and extension will not serve our purpose.

The difficulty here is actually rather more complicated and turns on the following facts: An extensional language can mention extensions but not intensions—its variables severally range over individuals, classes, and truth values. An intensional (i.e., modal) language can mention intensions but not extensions—its variables severally range over individual *concepts*, intensional properties, and intensional propositions. Thus in an intensional language one *can* mention the intension of 'Scott'. And so again we are forced to ask if there are not serious objections to modal logic. I have already echoed Quine's misgivings about the modalities. In chapter VI we shall find that we want G-propositions, modal operators or no. And I think the following consideration is quite decisive.

It is very likely that the intensions of 'Walter Scott' are different in the languages of each of us. If C4′ were a suitable elaboration of C3, it would mean that 'Walter Scott' has a different significance in each of our languages. And similarly for all our proper names. Then by C3 we use different languages and by C2 we should none of us succeed in intercommunicating. But we do intercommunicate. Therefore C4′ is not a suitable elaboration of C3. In other words, where extension gives us too lax a criterion of language identity, intension gives us too stringent a criterion.

If the foregoing argument against the use of the concept of intension seems shaky, it is because the whole notion of the intension of an individual constant is hopelessly obscure. For example, if it is maintained that the extension of a sign is secondary to its intension, because given the intension, an empirical investigation will enable us to discover the extension, then we should want to know what it would be like to know the intension of, say, 'Chicago' but not to know its extension. And we should want to know the empirical procedures by which we should pass from the intension to the extension. Of course, the problem here is going to arise in some form or another in any case, but we should allow ourselves a clear field in choosing methods to attack it. If the notion of the intension of an individual constant is obscure at this stage, that is all the more reason for declining to erect a system of general semantics on the concept of intension. Of course naming is pretty mysterious, but it seems to me to be less mysterious than the notion of the intension of an individual constant.

Nevertheless the reader will perhaps sense a kind of inconsistency here. Earlier, in raising objections to E-designation, we laid it down that 'Scott' and 'the author of *Waverley*' differ in significance in spite of having the same extension. Here we are laying it down that two names of the same individual would have the same significance even if they had different intensions. Although this procedure leaves the notion of *significance* very much up in the air, it is actually appropriate. In an earlier paper, *Proper Names*, I was concerned to show that names cannot be assimilated to descriptions. For a name and a description function in ways whose difference can be quite easily described. On that account we are justified in holding that they differ in significance. But as was noted, we have to take it that names do not signify by meaning (having an intension), they signify by naming (or, G-designating) as descriptions do not, and if two names name the same thing they have the same significance.

So far, I have been concerned to make it clear that we really are confronted with a Scylla and Charybdis. To navigate between them, we elaborate certain suggestions in Carnap's *M & N* (pp. 71–3).[9] We note that the intension of 'blue' (in English) and the extension of 'Walter Scott' are both *givable* (or directly mentionable). At any rate, at the common sense level, before we become preoccupied with semantic concepts, we should say that they are givable, and we shall make sure that we have a metalanguage in which they *are* givable. The intension of 'blue' and the extension of 'Walter Scott' are respectively the colour blue and the individual Walter Scott. So let us call these entities the respective *G-designata* of 'blue' and 'Walter Scott' (in English) and say that these expressions *G-designate* those entities respectively. ('*G*' for '*gives*'.) And we use a metalanguage of the sort described in §8. To escape the difficulty noted in connection with descriptions and E-designation, we stipulate that *descriptions do not G-designate* (they are not names).

Quite apart from present exigencies we should never in the first place have regarded descriptions as designating, or as names of, their descripta. Let us adopt the reasonable convention that a sentence is about just those entities which a person who understands the sentence knows it to be about. That is, a person who understands the sentence, 'Walter Scott is Scotch', knows that the sentence is about Scott and Scotchness, and the sentence *is* therefore about these entities. But George IV understood the sentence, 'The author of *Waverley* is Scotch', and did not know that it is about Scott. Therefore the sentence is *not* about, does not mention, Scott. Therefore there is no reason for regarding 'The author of *Waverley*' as a name of Scott.

Even after all that has been said 'G-designates' has not been defined and the concept of G-designation has certainly not been explicated. But before we undertake the definition there are certain general ontological questions that will have to be explored (in chapter IV). And sooner or later—it may as well be sooner—we shall have to take up the question of classes.

§15. CLASS EXPRESSIONS

The question of classes is a policy question: Shall we let them in or keep them out? We shall find it expedient to keep them out. Let us suppose that class expressions are introducible and eliminable simply

---

[9] This whole work is of course enormously indebted to Carnap, and I should regret it if this fact were obscured by the number of criticisms I have offered.

by definition. That is, definition alone is sufficient to enable us to pass from one to the other of

(16)   Scott is human,

(17)   Scott is a member of the class of humans.

In this case we shall have

(18)   'Scott is human' G-designates (in English always) that Scott is human,

and by definition we shall obtain

(19)   'Scott is human' G-designates that Scott is a member of the class of humans.

But in M:

(20)   The class of humans = the class of featherless bipeds.

Hence, by interchange in (19),

(21)   'Scott is human' G-designates that Scott is a member of the class of featherless bipeds.

And by definition again,

(22)   'Scott is human' G-designates that Scott is featherless-bipedal.

Now presumably we have

(23)   Human $\neq$ Featherless-bipedal

and, by Axiom 19,

(24)   Scott is human $\neq$ Scott is featherless-bipedal.

Statements (18), (22), (24), and the univocity axiom GAx1 (p. 29) are jointly self-contradictory. The occurrence of the contradiction—even under rather special conditions—should lead us to view classes with a certain amount of suspicion.

However, let us consider the case where the language contains class expressions as primitive together with axioms governing their use. Now it would require logical manipulation to get from (16) to (17) and by reason of the logical isolation of 'Scott is human' on the RHS of (18) we should not be able to derive (19) from (18) and for much the same reason we should not be able to derive (22) from (21). Thus we should not have a contradiction. But even now what are we to make of class expressions? Consider,

(20) the class of humans = the class of featherless bipeds.

The truth of this statement means that the LHS and RHS refer to the same entity. We should not say, however, that the LHS and the RHS have the same significance. And since G-designation is part of a reconstruction of significance we shall not want to say that both sides G-designate the same entity. We therefore say that they are descriptions of the same entity, namely, the class which would be G-designated by the class expression '{Adam, Eve, . . . , Scott, . . . }'[10] if the dotted portions were filled in with the names of all human beings. (I am following Carnap, *M & N*, §20.) And it would be plausible to suppose that the sentence, 'Scott is a member of the class of humans', describes the logically true proposition that Scott is a member of {Adam, Eve, . . . , Scott, . . .}, and that 'Scott is a member of {Adam, Eve, . . . , Scott, . . .}' G-designates the same proposition. And we should have, presumably,

(25) Scott is human ≠ Scott is a member of the class of humans.

For the LHS refers by G-designating to one proposition and the RHS refers by describing to a different one. We should require rules to enable us to prove (25), although they are more readily talked about than stated. Again, what would we do with the following?

(26) Scott is a member of {Adam, Eve, . . . , Scott, . . .} = Bucephalus is a member of {Bucephalus, . . . , Man o' War, Trigger, . . . }.

I do not see how we could manage to call this true. Yet if it were false we should have the anomaly of two logically equivalent sentences (the LHS and RHS are both logically true) G-designating distinct propositions. The anomalies are accumulating to the point where we shall have to consider seriously rejecting classes and class expressions. However, further considerations will come to light in the next chapter.

[10]Braces would be defined as follows (*M & N*, p. 83):
$$\{x_1, x_2, \ldots x_n\} =_{\text{df}} (\lambda y)(y = x_1 \lor y = x_2 \lor \ldots \lor y = x_n).$$

IV. THE ONTOLOGY OF G

§16. BACKGROUND: QUINE'S CRITERION

Our quest for a definition of language—or rather our quest for a suitable designation relation to use in defining 'language'—has already involved us in a fairly explicit ontological commitment. We shall now have to canvass the whole question of ontology in greater detail. It will turn out that our method requires not merely its own peculiar ontology but also a new ontological criterion. It is worth remarking that ontological questions—questions like 'Are there universals?' or 'Are there negative facts?' or 'Are there sense-data?' cannot be attacked frontally with any hope of success. Answers can be given only as corollaries in a fairly large system connected with some enterprise or other, usually the enterprise of framing an explicit definition of something. The validity of the ontological answer will depend on both the importance of the enterprise and its success. Furthermore, such answers are always provisional, since system gives way to system.

I believe I should be following Quine[1] if I said that ontology is concerned with the question, 'What is there?' We may define a prior field of *theoretical ontology* concerned with the question, 'How do you go about answering the preceding question?' That is to say, theoretical ontology is concerned to find an ontological criterion. Quine's criterion —'to be is to be the value of a variable'—is not a definition (existence, of course, is indefinable). We are being told simply that an inventory of all values of the variables of a language is the same as an inventory of all entities in the domain of that language.

This criterion is presumably arrived at by some line of reasoning such as the following: We cannot distinguish between existence and non-existence. (For we should then have two classes of entities, those entities which exist and those entities which do not exist—and, offhand at least, that would seem to be nonsense.) And so let us distinguish instead between those expressions which designate entities and those which do not. To begin with we note that expressions in argument places are replaceable by variables in inferences of existential generalization, the conclusion reading, "There *is* an entity such that . . . " And so we infer that any expression in an argument place designates an

[1] In his *Notes, Designation, On What.*

entity, unless it is a description, in which case it may not even refer indirectly to an entity. Now some entities will be designated by signs of the language, other entities of the same logical type will not have designators in the language, but they will be in the range of a replacing variable. Since we shall wish to include these latter in the ontology we do not say, "To be is to be designated," but rather, "To be is to be ranged over by a variable, that is, to be is to be the value of a variable." Next (and this goes beyond Quine) we may have quantifiable variables which occur in the predicate place. Their occurrence requires no alteration of the ontological criterion, since a value-expression of a predicate variable may always appear as the argument of an identity sentence. Thus the distinction between designative and non-designative is made to hinge only on the question of replaceability by a quantifiable variable and not on the question of place of occurrence.

Quine goes on to add that in determining the ontology of a given language we consider only sentences in primitive notation. If quantification over higher order variables is reducible through definition, then the higher ontological commitment is regarded merely as apparent, not as real. This qualification is important in that it enables Quine to arrive at a clear formulation of the task of the nominalist: to construct an adequate language in which all higher order quantification is eliminable.

It should be noted that even within ontology (as distinct from theoretical ontology) there are two kinds of procedure: first (*a priori* and general), a statement of the categories of existence, and second (*a posteriori* and specific), a listing of the entities in each category. In doing ontology we should thus have three steps. (1) The criterion, to be is to be the value of a variable. (2) The language in question contains (say) quantifiable individual variables and quantifiable first order predicate variables; therefore in respect to the language, there are individuals and there are properties of individuals. (3) If we were eager, we could proceed to a listing of the individuals and properties there are.

§17. A NEW THEORETICAL ONTOLOGY

The present method requires a certain amount of revision of the foregoing. At this point I shall have to take the reader into my confidence. He may have noted, somewhat uneasily, that the languages of G, as described in chapter III, are such as to make it difficult to get cardinal arithmetic into them in any kind of orthodox fashion, let alone to derive mathematics from logic. On this account some rather desperate expedients will have to be adopted in the Appendix. These require a new ontological criterion. But I do not wish to defend the ontological criterion merely by citing the desperate expedients necessary in the Appendix. I should rather defend it on general philosophical grounds and from some of the very basic commitments already made—commitments by no means peculiar to G. Then when we come to the Appendix the desperate expedients there will seem a little less desperate. The dialectic will take a rather ironic turn, because *with* the new ontological criterion, the objections of §15 to axiomatically introduced class expressions fall. And with class expressions an orthodox derivation of mathematics would be possible. Nevertheless, we adhere to the desperate expedients because the methods of the Appendix have a certain outrageous charm of their own (and some systematic merits).

The elementary ontology of G has already been made clear in chapter III. But there we freely decided not to recognize identity, molecular, or general propositions (and were thence more or less forced not to recognize properties defined in terms of the identity sign, connectives or quantifiers). That free decision will require some defence. The novel aspects of our theoretical ontology can be stated as follows: *Logical expressions are non-designative even if they are value expressions of a quantifiable variable and even if that quantification is not eliminable through definition.* We do not recognize numbers and, more generally, we do not recognize any *entia rationis.* Further (to recapitulate chapter III) any expression containing the identity sign, a connective or operator (quantificational, iota, or lambda), or defined in terms of these (i.e., any expression defined with the help of logical signs other than variables) is non-designative. (An expression defined with the help of an iota operator may be referential. See §12 (*e*).)

And now the argument.

(*a*) Suppose you are trying to explain the meaning (i.e., significance) of an expression of a language. There seem to be three cases. You might mention its designatum using an expression of an understood metalanguage. Or you might simply point to the individual in question or to an instance of the property in question. However you proceed, you are trying to convey a correlation of an expression to an entity. In the second case you are dealing with a defined descriptive expression. Here you simply say, "Such and such is a definition of the language," and then go on, if necessary, to explain the expressions occurring in the definiens. The third case has to do with logical expressions. You can explain a logical sign by syntactical rules. The sign '&' might be explained by saying that a full sentence of '&' with components S_1 and S_2 is logically implied by S_1 and S_2 jointly and logically implies each of S_1 and S_2. Leaving aside the second case for the moment (defined descriptive expressions) we have it that some simple primitive signs signify by being correlated with entities, others signify in virtue of the patterns of deductions into which sentences containing these signs enter. I am adopting the position that these are exclusive alternatives. If you can explain the meaning of the numeral '2', for example, by purely syntactical means, that is, without invoking any specific entity with which it is allegedly correlated, then there is no reason to suppose that there is such an entity. This is the general philosophical argument on behalf of the ontological criterion of G. Unfortunately, it is purely negative. It proves at most that we do not *have* to recognize *entia rationis*. It does not show that we must not.

(*b*) And so we have to ask if there are any reasons *against* supposing that there are entities correlated with logical signs. If the significance of an expression is explicable *both* by giving syntactical rules and by mentioning the entity it signifies (i.e., G-designates), what guarantee have we that these two characterizations of the significance of an expression coincide? For example, one can presumably frame a syntactical definition of what it is to be a '2' numeral, just as one can frame a syntactical definition of 'sign of conjunction'. How does one know that a '2' numeral designates the number 2? One can adopt the principle that a '2' numeral always designates the number 2 or the more general principle that an nth numeral always designates the number n. But where does this principle come from? Do we pull it out of the air, or is it synthetic *a priori*? A different procedure is suggested by R5 in chapter v, which, in effect, concedes that there may be certain structures in which the atomic sentences G-designate random propositions, but insists that these structures are not languages. If a structure is to be a language any of its atomic sentences must G-designate the proposition constituted by the designata of the components of that sentence. Here, the comparable procedure would be this: The principle regarding the designata of numerals would be incorporated into the definition of 'language' so that it would be, not synthetic *a priori*, but rather true by definition. But the fact that we should have to make a special stipulation regarding the designata of numerals indicates that *we should be free to make a different stipulation or no stipulation at all*. And the making of special provisions for the designation of numerals is extra labour to no purpose. It is much simpler to deny that numerals designate. Thus the present argument is an argument from laziness, and other things being equal, it seems to me that the appeal to laziness should carry great weight. The necessity of using R5 below does not justify a comparable procedure in the case of numerals but rather places us under heavy obligation to justify recognition of atomic propositions.

In denying the existence of numbers, I am not of course proposing to dispense with numerical variables and quantificational logic in arithmetic. This logic is kept intact but its apparent ontological commitment is regarded as a pretence even though quantification over numerical variables is not eliminable. We can, if we wish, say that numbers are pseudo-entities.

In the foregoing argument I was, in effect, advocating the following general principle:

A. If, in explaining the significance of an expression E, it is not necessary *at once* to mention a non-linguistic entity, then E is non-designative. (Exceptions in the case of simple defined predicates.)

The phrase 'at once' has reference to the second class of expressions mentioned in (a), namely, complex defined descriptive expressions and logically complex sentences. Suppose we wish to explain the significance of 'Q_1' defined as '$Q_1x =_{df} P_1x \lor P_2x$' where '$P_1$' and '$P_2$' can be presumed to be primitive and therefore designative. In explaining 'Q_1' we first state the definition and *then* (not "at once") explain 'P_1' and 'P_2' by mentioning their designata. The point is, we can explain 'Q_1' without invoking its alleged designatum, and therefore, according to our principle, we should judge 'Q_1' to be non-designative.

Now let us consider our general principle in relation to complex sentences (i.e., identity, molecular, or general sentences) and complex defined properties. By §12(c) these stand or fall together and therefore an argument against one is an argument against the other. The reason for renouncing complex propositions is much the same as that given in the case of the numerals. We can presumably frame a purely syntactical description of 'sign of conjunction' and of 'conjunction sentence'—to take just one example. How would we know that a conjunction sentence G-designates the proposition which is the conjunction of the propositions G-designated by the components of that conjunction sentence? Again we should have to go to the trouble of complicating our definition of 'language' with a number of rules governing the designation of complex sentences. And again we lend ear to the argument from laziness and decide that it would be preferable simply to deny that complex sentences and complex defined predicates designate. Statement A is simply an explicit statement of the principle which guides us.

Before we go on to considerations a bit more impressive than the argument from laziness (or, more euphemistically, methodological parsimony) we shall have to pause over the prefix 'pseudo'. I have already suggested that we can look upon numbers as being pseudo-entities, to put it in the material mode. In the formal mode, we should say that numerals pseudo-designate and numerical variables pseudo-range. Pseudo-ranging variables are of course to be distinguished from genuinely ranging variables. A variable genuinely ranges if at least one of its value expressions is designative, otherwise it pseudo-ranges. Since a first order first degree variable genuinely ranges, non-designative (i.e., complex defined) predicates may not appear as value expressions, nor may they appear in argument places (e.g., of identity sentences). But in the case of pseudo-ranging variables, no distinction need be observed between primitive and defined constants of the same type as that variable. All may serve as value expressions and may appear in argument places of identity sentences. Thus the identity sign has a certain dual function. (Its primary syntactical function is of course constant: it means universal interchangeability.) If we recognize an entity we can always say that it is self-identical. But a statement of self-identity may *or may not* indicate recognition of the corresponding entity. It depends on what kind of variable—genuinely ranging or pseudo-ranging—appears when we perform existential generalization to get 'There is an entity *e* such that *e* is identical with . . . '. It is because first order first degree variables are genuinely ranging that we cannot consistently *deny* that complex defined first order first degree constants designate an entity and at the same time permit them to serve as value expressions of that variable. If we were to say that such defined predicates pseudo-designate, then the foregoing remarks would be summarized as follows: a pseudo-designative expression is not a value expression of a genuinely ranging variable and may not appear in argument places if the variable of the same type genuinely ranges. If the variable pseudo-ranges then a pseudo-designative expression of the same type may serve as the value expression of that variable and may appear in argument places.

(*c*) Any argument for the ontological criterion of G which comes closer to being decisive than those already given will of course be contingent upon a much more specific set of assumptions. The following argument assumes recognition of properties (as distinct from classes) and in addition appeals to a methodological principle of non-arbitrariness.

If we are going to recognize molecular properties—negative, conjunctive, and disjunctive properties—then we ought to be able to recognize negative, conjunctive, and disjunctive individuals. Thus in analogy to the definitions of molecular properties:

$$Q_5x =_{df} \sim P_1x,$$
$$Q_6x =_{df} P_1x \;\&\; P_2x,$$
$$Q_7x =_{df} P_1x \lor P_2x,$$

we should have definitions of molecular individuals ('*F*' a predicate variable):

$$Fc =_{df} \sim Fa,$$
$$Fd =_{df} Fa \;\&\; Fb,$$
$$Fe =_{df} Fa \lor Fb.$$

Now let us define the negative individual '*c*' and four conjunctive properties:

D1. $Fc =_{df} \sim Fa.$
D2. $Q_1x =_{df} P_1x \;\&\; P_2x.$
D3. $Q_2x =_{df} \sim P_1x \;\&\; P_2x.$
D4. $Q_3x =_{df} P_1x \;\&\; \sim P_2x.$
D5. $Q_4x =_{df} \sim P_1x \;\&\; \sim P_2x.$

We may now prove a contradiction:

(1) $P_2a \lor \sim P_2a.$

(2) $P_2a.$
(3) $\sim(P_1a \;\&\; \sim P_2a)$ (2).
(4) $\sim(\sim P_1a \;\&\; \sim P_2a)$ (2).
(5) $\sim Q_3a$ (3), D4.
(6) $\sim Q_4a$ (4), D5.
(7) Q_3c (5), D1.
(8) Q_4c (6), D1.
(9) $P_1c \;\&\; \sim P_2c$ (7), D4.
(10) $\sim P_1c \;\&\; \sim P_2c$ (8), D5.
(11) $P_1c \;\&\; \sim P_1c$ (9), (10).

(12) $\sim P_2 a$.

(13) $\sim(P_1 a \ \& \ P_2 a)$.

Similarly, using 'Q_1' and 'Q_2'

(21) $P_1 c \ \& \sim P_1 c$.

(22) $P_1 c \ \& \sim P_1 c$ (1), (2)–(11), (12)–(21).

We may conclude that joint recognition of molecular individuals and molecular properties will give rise to contradictions. We may escape by arbitrarily accepting molecular individuals and renouncing molecular properties. Or, as is more usual, we may escape by arbitrarily accepting molecular properties and renouncing molecular individuals. But we should escape arbitrariness only by renouncing all molecular entities whatever. I am here invoking a kind of categorical imperative: Recognize only those entities whereby thou canst at the same time recognize all entities constructed in generally the same sort of way.

There is, of course, a fallacy in the preceding proof of contradiction. Line (7), '$Q_2 c$', is ambiguous; it expands into either '$\sim P_1 a \ \& \ P_2 a$' or '$\sim P_1 a \ \lor \ P_2 a$' depending on whether '$Q_3$' or '$c$' is eliminated first. However, let us consider the property form of Russell's Paradox. We define the property *impredicative*:

$$\text{Imp}(F) =_{df} \sim F(F).$$

The contradiction falls out easily:

(1) $\quad \text{Imp}(\text{Imp})$

(2) $\quad \sim\text{Imp}(\text{Imp})$ Df.

(3) $\quad \sim\text{Imp}(\text{Imp})$

(4) $\quad \text{Imp}(\text{Imp})$ Df.   –

(5) $\quad \text{Imp}(\text{Imp}) \equiv \sim\text{Imp}(\text{Imp})$.

Now it could be pointed out that this antinomy also depends on an ambiguity. If we may take it that restatement is a trivial form of expansion then the alleged sentence 'Imp(Imp)' may be expanded either as line (1) or as line (2). However, if an antinomy is to be interesting, it must be possible to develop it *without* the defined expressions. And to develop Russell's Paradox without using 'Imp' we require an abstraction axiom:

AbAx1. $\quad (\exists F)(x)(Fx \equiv \ldots x \ldots).$

("Whatever you say about an individual, it is the same as ascribing some single property to that individual.") This axiom is what would be called the justificatory sentence[2] of all definitions of molecular properties, in the sense that it justifies the practice of allowing defined predicates to serve as value expressions of variables. The analogue for individuals would be:

AbAx2. $(\exists x)(F)(Fx \equiv \ldots F \ldots)$.

("Whatever you say about any property, it is the same as ascribing that property to some single individual.") With both AbAx1 and AbAx2 we can get the original contradiction without definitions D1–5. And so these abstraction axioms are jointly self-contradictory. In an extensional language, where predicate variables in effect range over classes, AbAx1 can be taken to mean that whatever you say about any individual, it is the same as assigning that individual to some single class. With this interpretation, the axiom is plausible. But if the predicate variable in AbAx1 ranges over properties, then the axiom is not a bit more plausible than AbAx2. And since one of these axioms must go, it seems to me that we should discharge them both. As a consequence of giving up AbAx1 we shall have to refuse to allow complex defined predicates to serve as value expressions of variables. As an argument against complex defined properties, the foregoing is *pari passu* an argument against identity, molecular, and general propositions.

(*d*) I shall introduce the final attack on complex propositions by considering Church's proof (*Rev. Carnap*, p. 300) that sentences designate, not propositions, but truth values. Church uses an extensional designation relation, but we must assure ourselves that the same result—or other embarrassing results—would not be derivable with 'G-designates'. G-designation is saved by what I have been calling the logical isolation of sentences in argument places and by the fact that it is not the case that if a sentence G-designates a proposition then any logically equivalent sentence G-designates the same proposition.

The considerations adduced by Church, however, suggest a further argument against regarding molecular sentences as designative. It is one of those tiresomely intricate arguments, yet it is fairly important because it shows quite decisively that once we have committed our-

[2] Carl G. Hempel, *Concept Formation*, p. 18.

selves to the basic features of G, then *some* ontological economies must be effected to preserve consistency. (The basic features are recognition of some properties and rejection of the modalities.)

Let us make the reasonable assumption that if two logically equivalent sentences are both designative, they both G-designate the same proposition. Let us suppose further that we recognize the relation of identity, properties defined with logical signs (in particular the L-determinate properties such as *being identical with* a *or identical with* b) and complex propositions. Now we shall be able to produce a contradiction like that noted in connection with definitionally introduced class expressions in §15.

First it is necessary to define 'class-property'. I shall not use the phrase 'L-determinate property' because that phrase has rather special connotations of its own.

$$F \text{ is the null property} =_{df} Fx = (y)(y \neq x).$$

("To have F is the same as to be distinct from everything.")

$$F \text{ is the universal property} =_{df} Fx = (\exists y)(x = y).$$

("To have F is the same as to be identical with some individual.")

$$F \text{ is a unit property} =_{df} (\exists y)[Fx = (x = y)].$$

("There is an individual such that to have F is the same as to be identical with that individual.")

$$G \text{ and } H \text{ are property components of } F =_{df} Fx = (Gx \lor Hx).$$

The definition of 'class-property' is enumerative and recursive:

F is a class-property $=_{df}$ F is the null property or F is the universal property or F is a unit property or F has property components all of which are class-properties.

It is evident that according to the definition, P, defined as

$$Px =_{df} x = a \lor x = b \lor x = c$$

is a class-property, and Q, defined as

$$Qx =_{df} x = a \lor x \text{ is human}$$

is not a class-property.

Now with the generous ontology we were supposing we should have

(1) Scott is human,
(2) Scott has the class-property co-extensive with Human,

as logically equivalent and, supposing them both to be designative, they would G-designate the same proposition. Also

(3) 'Scott has the class-property co-extensive with Human' G-designates the proposition that Scott has the class-property co-extensive with Human.

But in M,

(4) the class-property co-extensive with Human is identical with the class-property co-extensive with Featherless-bipedal.

Hence, by interchange in (3),

(5) 'Scott has the class-property co-extensive with Human' G-designates the proposition that Scott has the class-property co-extensive with Featherless-bipedal.

As in the case of (1) and (2) we shall have

(6)   Scott is featherless-bipedal,

(7)   Scott has the class-property co-extensive with Featherless-bipedal,

as logically equivalent and therefore co-designative. Also,

(8) 'Scott has the class-property co-extensive with Featherless-bipedal' G-designates the proposition that Scott has the class property co-extensive with Featherless-bipedal.

Since co-designation is a transitive relation, and since (1) and (2) are co-designative and (6) and (7) are co-designative, then in virtue of (5) and (8), (1) and (6) are co-designative. But it would be easy to show (using the univocity axiom, GAx1 (above p. 29) and the fact that the proposition that Scott is human is not identical with the proposition that Scott is featherless-bipedal) that (1) and (6) are *not* co-designative. Hence the contradiction. Clearly, we cannot tolerate the generous ontology supposed at the beginning of this sub-section.

We have as our general ontological principle the rule: *ceteris paribus*, reject every entity that does not have to be invoked to explain significance. The arguments in favour of the principle have not been individually decisive, although collectively they may have a certain amount of weight. A motive for adopting the principle is a desire to simplify the main task in the next chapter. And there is also this rationale: we have just seen that systematic considerations within G require us to enforce some economies. It seemed desirable to find some general principle, arguable on general philosophic grounds—however inconclusively—which would independently justify these economies. The fact that our principle is stronger than strictly necessary to preserve consistency is not to the point. When we are faced with a choice between a heroic general principle and a timid *ad hoc* stipulation, then it seems to me that we should always choose the principle. It is true that there are exceptions to the general principle: we do recognize simple defined properties. (Hence the *ceteris paribus* clause in the statement of our rule.) But these exceptions are not gratuitous.

The situation regarding classes has altered. No class expression requires immediate mention of an entity to explain its significance. The lambda operator can be explained by purely syntactical methods. Therefore even L-determinate class expressions (i.e., those which list the membership of the class) are non-designative and class variables pseudo-range. Provided class expressions are introduced axiomatically and not by definition (see §15), we could admit sentences containing class expressions. But a sentence containing a class expression is non-designative (and non-referential) and may not appear in argument places (e.g., on the RHS of G-designation statements). The sentence, 'a is a member of the class of P's' is in much the same case as 'Pa & $(Qc \vee \sim Qc)$'. (See above, p. 36.) Thus some of the anomalies noted in the second part of §15 vanish, and there is no particular objection to axiomatically introduced class expressions. They will be excluded from the object languages of chapter v because their admission would gratuitously complicate a task already complicated enough. However, we shall require in the metalanguage expressions for classes of expressions and for sequences of expressions and for couples containing an expression and a non-linguistic entity. And since languages will be "composed" of classes and sequences, we have to conclude that languages are pseudo-entities and that language variables pseudo-range. But the question, 'What kind of pseudo-entity is a language?' remains and it is an important question.

The "general principle" which has been discussed is not the same as an ontological criterion. With one preliminary definition we may formulate the criterion as statement B.

Df. A genuinely ranging variable of a language is a variable any of whose value expressions is designative in that language.

(A general definition of 'designative' will be given as D4 in §19.)

B. To be (in the domain of a given language) is to be a value of a genuinely ranging variable (of that language).

In connection with our departure from Quine's criterion, it should be remarked that Quine's rule is syntactical: it issues *From a Logical Point of View*. The present criterion is semantical, since the notion of a genuinely ranging variable turns on the semantical notion of *designation*. It may well be that once we get into pragmatics we shall require still a different criterion.

V. THE DEFINITIONS

§18. ASSOCIATION

We shall require some metalinguistic apparatus for handling expressions. In his *Semantic Truth* (n. 5) Tarski writes, "For our present purposes it is somewhat more convenient to understand by 'expressions,' 'sentences,' etc., not individual inscriptions, but classes of inscriptions of similar form . . . . " Goodman and Quine (in *Steps*, p. 121) point out that on this view (with certain obvious assumptions) "shapes having no inscriptions as instances reduce to the null class and are thus identical." In his review of *Steps* F. B. Fitch points out that the foregoing criticism of Tarski's method simply shows that expressions should be treated as attributes rather than as classes.[1] The difficulty with inscription classes would be avoided since identity and difference of attributes in no way depends on their instances.[2] The method, G, is particularly receptive to Fitch's suggestion since G involves property-platonism anyway. And so I shall assume a domain of expressions, which are neither inscriptions nor inscription classes, but rather inscriptibles. I shall use 'E_1', 'E_2', etc. as constants referring to unspecified expressions and 'E', 'E_i', 'E_j', etc. as variables ranging over expressions. I shall also have occasion to use 'e', 'e_i', 'e_j', etc. as variables ranging over all entities. Some expressions are unitary and others are the result of combining two or more expressions. The names of complex expressions would be defined in terms of names of unitary expressions and a combining relation. Earlier we adopted the view that most defined expressions do not name. Nevertheless here we shall permit defined expression names to serve as value expressions. Thus the logic of expressions is rather a law unto itself. I dislike this situation but the only alternative would be to pursue *inscriptional* semantics and such a procedure would produce enormous and gratuitous complications in the following exposition.

The combining relation to be used is rather like the customary concatenation relation, but differs enough to merit a name of its own, "association". The difference is this: If two expressions are

[1] *Journal of Symbolic Logic*, vol. XII (1948), pp. 49–50.
[2] For the foregoing bit of dialectic I am indebted to R. M. Martin, *Concatenation*, p. 419.

combined, they *stay* combined (associated) even when the combination is incorporated into larger expressions. It is assumed that there is always enough object language punctuation to indicate association. I shall also assume that we may, without inconsistency, permit the sign of association to be of ambiguous degree. Thus we shall have, for example, meta-sentences like:

$$\mathscr{A}(E_1, E_2, E_3), \qquad \mathscr{A}(E_1, E_2, E_3, E_4).$$

These are to be read as "E_1 is the association of E_2 and E_3 in that order" and "E_1 is the association of E_2, E_3 and E_4 in that order." It will be convenient to use Russell's definition of descriptive phrases (*PM*, *30.01) to define 'the association of . . .'.

AD1. $\mathscr{A}'(E_1, E_1, \ldots, E_n) =_{dt} (\imath E)[\mathscr{A}(E, E_1, E_1, \ldots, E_n)]$.

The metalinguistic symbol '$\mathscr{A}$' is primitive, but we have the following axioms for association:

AAx1. $E!\mathscr{A}'(E_1, E_1, \ldots, E_n)$.

("The association of a sequence of expressions is an expression and there is precisely one expression which is the association of a sequence of expressions.")

AAx2. $\mathscr{A}'(E_1, \ldots, E_m) = \mathscr{A}'(E_1, \ldots, E_n)$ if and only if $E_1 = E_1$ and . . . and $E_m = E_n$.

It follows from AAx2 that

$$\mathscr{A}'(E_1, E_2, E_3) \neq \mathscr{A}'(E_1, \mathscr{A}'(E_2, E_3)),$$
$$\mathscr{A}'(E_1, E_2, E_3) \neq \mathscr{A}'(\mathscr{A}'(E_1, E_2), E_3),$$
$$\mathscr{A}'(E_1, \mathscr{A}'(E_2, E_3)) \neq \mathscr{A}'(\mathscr{A}'(E_1, E_2), E_3).$$

We shall require also the definitions:

AD2. E_1 is a proximate component of $E_k =_{dt} E_1$ is a term of a sequence such that E_k is the association of the terms (in order) of that sequence.

AD3. E_1 is a component of $E_k =_{dt} E_1$ is a proximate component of E_k or E_1 is a component of a component of E_k.

AD4. E_1 is a unitary expression $=_{dt}$ there are no expressions other than E_1 itself which are components of E_1.

AD5. E_1 is an ultimate component of $E_k =_{dt} E_1$ is a unitary expression and is a component of E_k.

It will be convenient to eliminate the symbol '$\mathscr{A}$'. Instead of using the slur which normally denotes concatenation, we shall simply use no symbol at all. This convention is effected by the following definition:

AD6. $\qquad E_1 E_j \ldots E_n =_{df} \mathscr{A}{}'(E_1, E_j, \ldots, E_n)$
$\qquad \ldots (E_1 E_j \ldots E_n) \ldots =_{df} \ldots \mathscr{A}{}'(E_1, E_j, \ldots, E_n) \ldots$

Now the three above cited consequences of AAx2 would be written:

$$E_1 E_2 E_3 \neq E_1(E_2 E_3),$$
$$E_1 E_2 E_3 \neq (E_1 E_2) E_3,$$
$$E_1(E_2 E_3) \neq (E_1 E_2) E_3.$$

The point of our odd association relation is that it will enable us to avoid bogging down in matters pertaining to punctuation and will thereby simplify some of the subsequent definitions.

I wish now to introduce the notion of a multiply ranging expression variable. Throughout most of the exposition to follow we shall be dealing with *structures*, entities of the same type as languages. (All languages are structures but not all structures are languages.) The symbols 'St', 'St_1', 'St_j' etc. will be used as variables ranging over structures. At a certain point we shall define what it is to be a sentence of a structure. If St_1 is a specific structure, then we might use 'S' as a restricted expression variable ranging over all and only the sentences of St_1. Thus '$(S) \ldots$' would be understood to mean '$(E)(E$ is a sentence of $St_1 \supset \ldots)$' and '$(\exists S) \ldots$' to mean '$(\exists E)(E$ is a sentence of St_1 & $\ldots)$'. Now if we let St_1 vary, then 'S' becomes what might be called a doubly varying variable: it has an immediate range but the range varies from structure to structure. In the same way, once we have defined 'variable' we shall use 'v' as a restricted expression variable ranging over the variables of St. We shall use 'S_v' as a trebly varying variable ranging over the open sentences of St containing v as their sole freely occurring variable. It has an immediate range which varies first from variable to variable within the structure in question and secondly from structure to structure. Once we have defined 'implication sign', 'negation sign' and 'identity sign' we shall use '$\supset$', '$\sim$', and '$=$' as expression variables. (!) In the case of these variables the immediate ranges comprise just one expression but the ranges vary from structure to structure. The signs '$\supset$' and '$\sim$' may also be used as connectives in the metalanguage but there is no danger of ambiguity. For as connectives they are always associated with sentences and as expression variables they are always associated with other expression variables or constants. We shall also find it convenient to use 'B_1', 'B_j' etc. as variables ranging over the binary connectives of *St*. Once the quantifiers have been defined we shall use 'Q' as a variable ranging over just the quantifiers of the structure in question, 'Q_v' as a variable ranging over the quantifiers containing the variable v, and '(v)' and '$(\exists v)$' as variables ranging over the universal and existential quantifiers containing the variable v. Again, these last two have an immediate range of only one expression but the range varies with v and with *St*.

The use of an unsymbolized association relation (in '$\sim S$' below, for example) and of multiply ranging expression variables will permit us to say things such as:

If $\sim S$ is logically true in *St* then S is logically false in *St*.

$(\exists v)(S_v)$ is derivable in *St* from every instance of S_v.

Written out in full these would be:

If E_j is a sentence of *St* and if E_1 is the negation sign of *St*, then if $\mathscr{A}'(E_1, E_j)$ is logically true in *St*, E_j is logically false in *St*.

If v is a variable of *St* and if E_1 is the existential quantifier of *St* containing v and if E_j is an open sentence of *St* containing a free occurrence of the variable v, then $\mathscr{A}'(E_1, E_j)$ is derivable in *St* from every instance of E_j.

At the very least, our conventions would appear to contribute to clarity and conciseness.

Nevertheless the reader is perhaps a little baffled and/or bored by all the foregoing, and so a few additional remarks may be in order. If we are going to talk about specific expressions, then we can get along simply with the use of quotation marks. But when it comes to talking about *any* (unspecified) expression composing in a *specified* way another unspecified expression, then we require a much more elaborate apparatus, such as Carnap's sign-designs or Quine's quasi-quotes. And when it comes to talking about unspecified expressions *in an unspecified language* (as is necessary to do in general semantics) then we can expect still further complications to crowd in upon us. The method just outlined is intended to satisfy three requirements: (i) it should be serviceable in general semantics, (ii) it should provide a metalinguistic *façon de parler* which will be reasonably easy to read, and (iii) the explanation of this *façon de parler* should make sense under close scrutiny.

§19. 'G-DESIGNATES'

We are now ready to start work. It will be recalled that, however odd our procedure may seem, we are going to have to define 'language' in such a way that any specific language is definable without using semantic terms (i.e., definable prior to the definition of semantic terms for that language). This procedure arises from the necessity of avoiding the double elimination difficulty. Another oddity stems from the fact that we shall have to use both syntactical *and* semantical methods and shift from one to the other according to the exigencies of the situation. I shall appropriate Quine's distinction (*Dogmas*, pp. 26–7) between the primitive notation of a language and the language with its definitional superstructure, and I shall confine myself to defining 'language in primitive notation'. This restriction aims at keeping our task within reasonable limits. But I shall sometimes allude to defined expressions and such allusions will have the purpose of leaving room for certain defined expressions in case we wished eventually to extend the definition of 'language'. It was noted in §5 that in defining 'language' we shall have to assign a type to the word 'language' and then impose requirements which will differentiate languages from non-languages of the same type.

As a beginning, we may note that as Carnap defines 'designates' for L_1 (or 'designates-in-L_1'), the definition effects a mapping of expressions onto extra-linguistic entities. In the beginning, Carnap is using an extensional metalanguage and so the entities available for the mapping are extensions—individual, classes, and truth values. Since here we wish a mapping by which we can eventually define 'G-designates', we use a metalanguage of the sort described in chapter III, that is, one whose variables range over individuals, G-properties (of whatever type), and G-propositions. Let us say provisionally that an object language *is* the mapping—that is, a class of couples, the first term of each couple being an expression, the second, the entity mapped.

Now we have something that is beginning to look like part (ii *a*) of convention C4 (above, p. 22). We might call it the *descriptive part* of the language. What we want now is something that will take care of (ii *b*) of C4. That is, we shall lay a second term—the *logical part*— beside our mapping so that the language will be a couple of some kind or other. The logical part will consist of all the logically true sentences of the language and all possible *modus ponens* derivations of the language. I am leaping ahead at this point, but it will do no harm to give the reader an idea of how a structure (and therefore a language) will eventually look:

$$\left(\begin{array}{ll} \overbrace{\begin{array}{l} (E_1;e_1), \\ (E_2;e_2), \\ (E_3;e_3), \\ \ldots, \\ \ldots, \\ \ldots. \end{array}} & \overbrace{\begin{array}{l} E_\mathrm{a}, \\ E_\mathrm{b}, \\ \ldots, \\ (E_\mathrm{p};E_\mathrm{q};E_\mathrm{r}), \\ (E_\mathrm{s};E_\mathrm{t};E_\mathrm{u}), \\ \ldots. \end{array}} \end{array} \right)$$

Braces and commas are used to indicate classes, parentheses and semi-colons to indicate couples. With these few tentative suggestions we may now begin imposing the requirements which will differentiate languages from non-languages. We shall use the term 'structure' for entities of the general type and we shall use 'St', 'St_1', 'St_j' as variables ranging over all structures. All the requirements given are to be understood as prefaced by the phrase, 'A structure St is a language only if . . . . '. And if a structure satisfies all the requirements, then presumably it is a language.

R1. St is a couple whose first term is a non-empty class of couples, each couple comprising an expression and an extra-linguistic entity in that order, and whose second term is a class comprising expressions and triples of expressions.

The following definitions will be useful:

D1. The DP (descriptive part) of a structure St is the first term of St.

D2. The LP (logical part) of a structure St is the second term of St.

Obviously we do not wish to regard every class of couples as a descriptive part of a language and so we shall have to begin imposing the first of a long series of further requirements.

R2. The DP of St comprises a finite number of couples.

R3. The DP of St is at worst a many-one, not a one-many or a many-many mapping. (Maybe synonyms, but no homonyms.)

R4. Every expression of the DP of St either maps onto a (G-) proposition or is a component of an expression which maps onto a proposition in St. (No "isolated" designative expressions.)

If we were going to deal explicitly with descriptions we should require a syntactical characterization of descriptions and a stipulation to the effect that descriptions do not appear in the mapping. We may now define 'G-designates':

D3. E G-designates e in St $=_{df}$ the couple $(E;e)$ is a member of the DP of St.

D4. E is designative, or, is a designator, in St $=_{df}$ there is an e such that E G-designates e in St.

I shall take it that 'G-designates' is of type ω, and that e is a typeless variable ranging over all entities. (*Cf.* Carnap, *Semantics*, p. 51.) Since *defined* expressions for the most part are not value expressions of the variable e, there is no danger of contradictions arising. It will be noted also that all our definitions have to be framed in terms of structures. Once we have arrived at our definition of 'language' we can go back to the key definitions and replace 'St' by 'L'.

§20. 'ATOMIC SENTENCE'

At this point we shall have to give a brief, general glance at the logical part. What we want in the LP of a language is all of what will eventually be defined as the logically true sentences of the language. That is to say, we should specify the composition of the LP of a certain language by the enumerative and recursive methods customarily used in syntax to define 'provable' (for a given calculus). Since the specification of a set of sentences as logically true does not, without a deduction rule, fully determine the meanings of the logical signs, we shall have to include in the LP a class of sequences corresponding to *modus ponens* derivations. It is purely a matter of convenience that I am arbitrarily settling on the MP rule. Thus we should have what I shall call 'member expressions' of the LP and 'member triples' of the LP. The terms of the triples will be called 'triple-members'. Since every sentence is part of some *modus ponens* deduction or other we should have all and only sentences of L as triple-members of the LP of L.

Now it is fairly clear how, with a tendentious reading of rules of the sort used in §8, we should set about specifying (enumeratively and recursively) the composition of the language in question. The definition of L_2 would run as follows: L_2 is a couple. The first term of L_2 is the following class of couples: {('a'; New York), ('b'; Chicago), ('c'; the sky), ('P'; Large), . . .,('Pa'; New York is large), ('Pb'; Chicago is large), . . .}. The second term of L_2 is a class of expressions and triples of expressions. The triples are of the form $(E_1 \supset E_j; E_1; E_j)$ where E_1 satisfies the following conditions: there is a proposition p such that $(E_1; p)$ is a member of the first term of L_2, or there is an expression E_k which is a triple-member of L_2 and $E_1 = \sim E_k$, or there are expressions E_k and E_1, both triple-members of L_2, and $E_1 = E_k \supset E_1$ or $E_1 = E_k \& E_1$ or . . . etc., and where E_j satisfies the same conditions. An expression member E of the second term of L_2 satisfies the following condition: E is a triple-member of the second term of L_2 and is of one of the following forms: $E_1 \supset (E_j \supset E_1)$, etc. (see the axioms given in §8), or there are expressions E_j and E_k, both expression members of the second term of L_2, such that the triple $(E_j; E_k; E)$ is a member triple of the second term of L_2.

It will be noted that in characterizing L_2, we have not used any of the terms, 'sentence', 'axiom', 'designates', 'logically true'. Now although it is easy to see how one would specify the composition of any given language, what must be shown is how the return passage would be made. It must be shown how an infinite mind, confronted with the infinite composition of a language, could pack up all the characteristics of that language and present us with a finite, "acceptable" definition. The infinite mind here is simply a heuristic device to enable us to find the further requirements necessary to differentiate languages from non-languages. If, in the case of any given structure, the infinite mind can't do the trick, we shall say that the structure in question is not a language. We shall begin with a simple definition of 'sentence' and then impose the restrictions which will give us what we want in the way of a definition of 'sentence of language L'.

D5. *E is a sentence of St* $=_{dt}$ E is a triple-member of the LP of St.

For the time being we shall concentrate on atomic sentences.

D6. *E is an atomic sentence of St* $=_{dt}$ E G-designates a (G-) proposition in St.

In view of the fact that identity sentences are not designative in M and therefore not allowed to appear on the RHS of G-designation statements (i.e., there are no identity propositions to serve as ultimate factors of a DP of a structure), D6 is a narrower definition than usual: identity sentences of a language are not regarded as atomic in G. The reason is that identity sentences contain the identity sign, which is not designative. The reason is not that some identity sentences are analytic. As a matter of fact we do recognize the propositions that

red is a colour, that red is between orange and purple, and so on,
even though these might be regarded as analytic propositions. The
corresponding sentences of *M* may appear on the RHS of G-designation statements and there may be object language sentences mapped
onto these propositions. The reason for recognizing these propositions
is this: Assuming that certain higher order predicates (like 'colour'
and 'between') are primitive, then sentences applying these predicates
to first order properties are rather mysterious. They are not *obviously*
analytic or *obviously* synthetic. Provisionally, then, we may as well
do what we please with them until it is possible to become clearer
about them. And when it comes to the type restrictions, it happens
to be convenient to suppose that sentences containing higher order
primitive descriptive predicates are designative.

It will be noted, too, that we have reversed the usual roles of
'proposition' and 'sentence' in relation to one another. It is customary
to define 'sentence' by formation rules and then define 'proposition'
(in a loose sense of 'define') as 'what is expressed by a sentence.'
Here we are defining 'sentence'—or at least 'atomic sentence'—in
terms of 'proposition'. At this point we have no alternative, but the
ultimate rationale behind the manœuvre will become clearer in
chapter VI, where it will be argued that it is the world, not the semanticist, which lays down the atomic formation rules. An atomic fact
has a certain degree of complexity and this complexity must be
mirrored in the structure of atomic sentences. The "nature" of
propositions is prior to language and formation rules must take their
cue from that nature. In saying that at this point we have no alternative but to define 'atomic sentence' in terms of 'proposition', I have
in mind the argument to be given shortly *against* laying it down that
an individual constant is an expression which G-designates an individual. This argument is, by implication, also an argument against
defining 'predicate' as 'an expression which G-designates a property',
and then defining 'sentence' by formation rules. The *bouleversement*
here is perhaps important: for 'sentence' we are in semantics and for
'individual constant' and 'predicate constant' we move back into
syntax.

What has just been said has nothing to do with type theory, and
the adoption of type restrictions requires a separate rationale. They
are not required to preserve consistency, because our object languages
do not contain class expressions, nor an abstraction axiom for properties, and none but the most innocuous of predicates are permitted as
value expressions of variables. Hence the logical antinomies cannot

occur. Like Quine I feel that type theory for classes is counter-intuitive. But I feel that type theory for properties does make sense and is grounded in some kind of objective nature of things. My semi-final remarks on type theory—sufficient, I believe, to justify its adoption here—are made below (p. 133). However the rationale to be offered for type theory is not such as to militate against the use of typeless variables and a typeless identity sign.

Having defined an atomic sentence as an expression which G-designates a proposition we shall now want some kind of regularity requirement—something corresponding to the ordinary rule that a sentence of the form *PrIn* G-designates the proposition that what *In* G-designates has what *Pr* G-designates.[3] Without such a rule we might have 'Socrates' and 'unicorn' supplied with expected designation rules, but the sentence 'Socrates is a unicorn' G-designating the proposition that Chicago is large. And since Chicago *is* large, 'Socrates is a unicorn' would be true but would logically imply the false sentence, 'Something is a unicorn'. Yet it is not easy to get a suitable regularity requirement. We might stipulate that if *St* is to be a language every component of an atomic sentence *E* of *St* must G-designate a constituent of the proposition G-designated by *E* in *St*. This restriction would not suffice, because it would permit the expression 'New York is larger than' to be mapped onto the proposition that New York is larger than Chicago. On the other hand we cannot insist that for every constituent of the proposition there should be a corresponding expression in the atomic sentence. The reason is this: Presumably 'smaller than' would be defined in terms of 'larger than' without connectives or quantifiers. Hence the proposition that New York is larger than Chicago is identical with the proposition that Chicago is smaller than New York. (See above, p. 36.) Thus both the relation Larger Than and its converse, Smaller Than, are constituents of the proposition in question—being mutual supernumeraries, as it were. We do not want our atomic sentences to contain expressions for both of such mutually supernumerary constituents. And so we impose the following rather elaborate requirement:

R5. If E is an atomic sentence of St, G-designating in St the proposition p, then there are expressions E_1, E_j, . . . , E_n of St such that $E = E_1 E_j \ldots E_n$ (i.e., $E = \mathscr{A}'(E_1, E_j, \ldots, E_n)$) and there are entities e_1, e_j, . . . , e_n such that $p = e_1(e_j, \ldots, e_n)$ and E_1 G-designates e_1 in St and E_j G-designates e_j in St and . . . and E_n G-designates e_n in St.

[3] See, e.g., Carnap, *Semantics*, p. 51, rule *a*.

If—as is unlikely—the use of typeless variables in '$p = e_1(e_1, \ldots, e_n)$' engendered difficulties, then we could use variables *of variable type*, as in

$$'p = e_1{}^{(t_1 \cdots t_n)}(e_1{}^{t_1}, \ldots, e_n{}^{t_n}).$$

In this case a set of constants would be eligible or ineligible *en bloc* for substitution. This device might be useful in systems stronger than the present one (i.e., in systems strong enough to justify anxiety about the occurrence of antinomies), where it is desired to conform generally to the simplified theory of types and at the same time have resources for talking about all entities.

The definitions and requirements to follow have to do with the classification of signs and type restrictions. This question will arise: If you are going to say, "An atomic sentence is an expression which G-designates a proposition," then why can you not say, "An individual constant is an expression which G-designates an individual"? The answer is that, assuming we do not want to confine ourselves to object languages of the same general sort, then propositions and individuals are not in the same case. If an entity is a proposition, that is the end of the matter. If it is present in the domain of a given language then it is a proposition in the domain of that language. The same is not true of individuals. You may have a language whose individuals are what we should normally regard as first order properties and whose first order properties include properties like *the property of being exemplified in* a, *the property of being exemplified in* b, etc. Such a language could be adequate for normal purposes. Obviously an entity may be an individual of this language and be present in the domain of, but not an individual of, another language. If we are going to have object languages of different kinds then presumably our metalanguage will have to be a sum of languages of these kinds.[4] In such a case we should have in M no unequivocal notion of *individual*. For this reason we shall have to seek a purely syntactical characterization of what it is to be an individual constant of a structure.

D7. The *predicate place* of an atomic sentence E of St is the place of the first ultimate component of E.

D8. An *argument place* of an atomic sentence E of St is a place occupied by any component expression of E other than the first.

[4]The two main kinds I have in mind are space-time languages and substance languages as explained in my paper, *Space*. (The first are roughly comparable to Carnap's co-ordinate languages, the second are just Carnap's thing languages.)

R6. There are designative expressions of St which occur only in argument places of atomic sentences of St.

D9. E is an *individual constant* of St (or, E is of order 0 in St) $=_{dt}$ St satisfies R6 and E is a designative expression of St which occurs only in argument places of atomic sentences of St. (*Cf.* Aristotle, *Cat.* 2a11: "Substance . . . is that which is neither predicable of a subject nor present in a subject.")

D10. E_i is *of higher order* than E_j in St $=_{dt}$ E_i and E_j are both designative in St and there is an atomic sentence of St containing E_i in the predicate place and E_j in an argument place or there is an expression E_k of St such that E_i is of higher order than E_k in St and E_k is of higher order than E_j in St.

D11. E_i is *of order one higher* than E_j in St $=_{dt}$ E_i is of higher order than E_j in St and there is no expression E_k of St such that E_i is of higher order than E_k in St and E_k is of higher order than E_j in St.

R7. Every designative expression of St other than atomic sentences has an order. (That is, D9–11 shall provide an enumerative and recursive definition of *the* order of a designative expression.)

D12. E is *of degree n* in St $=_{dt}$ E is designative in St but not of 0 order and not an atomic sentence and every sentence of St containing E in the predicate place has n designative expressions in the argument places.

R8. Every designative expression of St other than individual constants or atomic sentences has a degree. (That is, if ever it occurs in a sentence of St with n arguments then it always occurs with n arguments.)

D13. E_i and E_j are *of the same type* in St $=_{dt}$ E_i and E_j are both atomic sentences of St or both individual constants of St or they are of the same degree and order in St and for every atomic sentence E_k and E_l of St having E_i and E_j in their respective predicate places, the nth argument of E_k is of the same type as the nth argument of E_l.

R9. Every designative expression of St is of unambiguous type.

R10. If E_i is an atomic sentence of St and E_j is an expression obtained from E_i by replacing a designative expression E_k of E_i by a designative expression E_l of the same type in St as E_k, then E_j is also an atomic sentence of St. (The generality requirement: The class of atomic sentences of St is to include all combinations of designators of St permitted by type theory.)

The requirements laid down are actually not independent. Type restrictions are effectively imposed by R5. For example, an object structure expression like 'Hard(Brown)' would violate R5. There is no proposition containing Hard and Brown in that order. If type theory has some objective basis in the nature of things then we should expect type restrictions to be imposed by R5. The immediate source of the restrictions is of course the metalanguage. When we say that there is no proposition containing Hard and Brown in that order it is a question whether we do not mean simply that 'Hard (Brown)' is not a sentence of the metalanguage. But if there is an "objective nature of propositions" then a metalanguage, to be usable, must reflect that nature. At any rate R6–9 are not independent of R5, but their derivation from R5 would require an argument in the metametalanguage which appeals to the structure of the metalanguage.

What is accomplished by R6–9 is this: We guarantee that an infinite mind, surveying just the atomic sentences of a structure which qualifies as a language, could, in principle, arrive at a classification of the primitive descriptive signs of that structure.

§21. 'SENTENCE'

Again we cross over to the logical part, this time with the intention of staying. D5 is worth repeating.

D5. E is a sentence of $St =_{df} E$ is a triple-member of the LP of St.

What we want now is something comparable to the formation rules of the sentential calculus. As the basis of a set of recursive requirements we impose the following:

R11. Every atomic sentence of St is a sentence of St (i.e., by D5, is a triple-member of St).

Now we can deal with some of the logical signs. So far as I know it is not possible to get what we want in the way of a definition of 'language' without a few fairly specific stipulations regarding the presence of certain specific signs.

R12. There is precisely one unitary sign Id of St (by definition the *identity sign* of St), such that if E_i and E_j are designative expressions of St of the same type or are atomic sentences of St, then $E_i Id E_j$ (i.e., $\mathscr{A}'(E_i, Id, E_j)$) is a sentence of St.

D14. *E* is an identity sentence of *St* $=_{dt}$ *E* is a sentence of *St* formed with the identity sign of *St* as in R12.

R13. There is precisely one unitary sign *Imp* of *St* (by definition, the *implication sign* of *St*), such that for every triple *T* of expressions of *St*, *T* is a member triple of the LP of *St* if and only if there are expressions E_1 and E_j which qualify independently as sentences (and atomic sentences of *St* so qualify), such that $T = ((E_1 \text{ Imp } E_j); E_1; E_j)$.

R14. There is precisely one sign *Neg* of *St* (by definition the *negation sign* of *St*), such that if *E* qualifies independently as a sentence of *St*, then *NegE* is a sentence of *St* (i.e., appears as a triple-member of the LP of *St*.

R15. (Not really a restriction but a licence.) The structure may contain signs B_1, B_j, . . . (which, along with the implication sign of *St* are, by definition, the *binary connectives* of *St*), such that if E_1 and E_j qualify independently as sentences of *St* then $E_1 B_1 E_j$, $E_1 B_j E_j$, etc. also qualify as sentences of *St*.

There is a simple requirement which may be introduced here even though it refers to signs not yet defined.

R16. The identity sign of *St*, the implication sign of *St*, the negation sign of *St*, the binary connectives of *St* other than the implication sign, the quantifier marks and variables of *St* are all distinct from one another and from the designative signs of *St*.

Having defined the identity, implication, and negation signs of *St* we shall now use '=', '⊃', and '∼' as multiply varying variables ranging over the identity sign, the implication sign, and the negation sign of *St* respectively, as explained in §18. The expressions 'B_1' and 'B_j' will be used as multiply varying variables ranging over the binary connectives of *St*.

We may now provide for the functional calculus.

R17. The structure *St* contains certain non-designative signs (by definition, the *variables* of *St*) which fall into certain classes as to type, and which are such that the result of replacing a designator in a sentence by a variable of the same type is a sentence.

(What is meant in speaking of the variables "falling into certain classes as to type" is this: if a certain atomic sentence remains a sentence when a designator is replaced by a variable, then no atomic sentence remains a sentence when a designator of a different type is replaced by that same variable.)

R18. The structure *St* contains certain complex signs (by definition, the *quantifiers* of *St*) which (i) are of two main kinds—later to be defined as universal and existential—and (ii) are composed of the common mark of that kind and a variable of *St*, and (iii) are such that if E_j is a sentence of *St* and E_1 a quantifier of *St*, then E_1E_j is a sentence of *St*.

R19. No expression is a sentence of *St* (i.e., appears as a triple-member of the LP) unless it so qualifies under R1-18.

As earlier explained, we shall now use 'Q' and 'v' as multiply ranging variables ranging over the quantifiers and variables of *St* respectively. The following definitions will be useful subsequently.

D15. E_j is the *scope* of (the quantifier) Q in E_1 in *St* $=_{dt}$ QE_j is either identical with E_1 or with a component of E_1.

D16. Variable v is *bound* in its nth occurrence in E in *St* $=_{dt}$ the nth occurrence of v in E is within the scope of a quantifier Q of E having v as its variable.

D17. Variable v is *free* in its nth occurrence in E in *St* $=_{dt}$ v is not bound in its nth occurrence in E.

D18. E is an *open sentence* of *St* $=_{dt}$ E is a sentence of *St* containing at least one free occurrence of a variable.

D19. E is a *closed sentence* of *St* $=_{dt}$ E is a sentence of *St* which is not open.

It might be noted in passing that 'A' falls outside the scope of the quantifier in '$(\exists x)(Fx) \lor A$', for that expression is $('(\exists x)''(Fx)')$ '$\lor$' 'A', *not* '$(\exists x)$'$('Fx' '\lor' 'A')$, as is '$(\exists x)(Fx \lor A)$'. The association relation originally chosen was expressly designed to make possible a simple definition of scope.

It is worth pausing to notice that a sentence falls into one of four main classes. It is atomic if it contains no logical signs (and incidentally if it G-designates a proposition). It is an identity sentence if it contains the identity sign but no connectives or quantifiers. It is general if its first component is a quantifier and everything else is within the scope of that quantifier. It is molecular if it is none of the first three. A molecular sentence has what will be called a *major connective* and either one (where the major connective is the negation sign) or two (where the connective is binary) proximate sentential components. These proximate sentential components may be of any of the four kinds. If molecular, then there will be proximate sentential components of the (molecular) proximate sentential components. An ultimate sentential component of a molecular sentence is a non-molecular component of that sentence.

There is also a cross classification into open and closed sentences. Open sentences are of the four kinds already mentioned: atomic (e.g., 'Px'), identity ('$x = a$'), general ('$(x)(Px \lor Qy)$'), or molecular ('$Px \lor Qy$'). These two classifications will be useful to us subsequently. Having defined what it is to be a sentence of St, we shall use 'S', 'S_1', 'S_j', etc. as variables ranging over just the *sentences* of St. We shall also use 'S_v' as a variable trebly ranging over the open sentences of St having a free occurrence of the variable v.

§22. 'LOGICALLY TRUE' AND 'LANGUAGE'

So much for the formation rules. We have specified the features which the class of member triples of the LP of a structure must have if that structure is to qualify as a language. We may now deal with the member expressions of the LP.

R20. Every member expression of St is a sentence of St.

And now a simple definition of 'logically true':

D20. S is *logically true* in St $=_{df}$ S is a member expression of the LP of St.

We can dispose of a few simple matters at this point.

D21. S is *logically false* in St $=_{df}$ $\sim S$ is logically true in St.

D22. S is *logically determinate* in St $=_{df}$ S is either logically true in St or logically false in St.

D23. S is *logically indeterminate* in St $=_{df}$ S is not logically determinate in St.

Now we shall want to begin to impose those further requirements on the class of expression members of the LP so that we can eventually replace 'St' by 'L' in D20 and have a suitable definition of 'S is logically true in L'. R21 (with D21) guarantees that our languages shall be

Aristotelian (i.e., two-valued) and R22 guarantees that they shall be consistent.

R21. $\sim S$ is logically false in St if and only if S is logically true in St.

R22. No sentence of St is both logically true and logically false in St.

We may at this point get the logically true identity sentences out of the way.

R23. Every identity sentence of St with identical designative arguments is logically true in St.

With R23 we have sentences like 'Tully = Tully' as logically true but not sentences like 'Tully = Cicero'. The latter is at most descriptively analytic and perhaps even synthetic. The qualification, 'designative' also rules out sentences like 'The king of France in 1905 = the king of France in 1905' because the *description* 'the king of France in 1905' is not designative.

We come now to more difficult matters. There are three conditions we shall want to impose. (i) We shall want a uniformity requirement: if any sentence of a certain form is logically true (or logically false) then every sentence of that form is logically true (or logically false). (ii) We shall want to be able to generate all logically true non-Gödelian sentences of St by means of chains of direct derivations from a finitely describable sub-class of the logically true sentences of St. (Of course, there may be any number of sub-classes having the required property, that is, any number of suitable axiom sets.) (iii) Finally, we shall want some kind of completeness requirement. Without this last, we should have no guarantee of there being enough logically true sentences in the language to enable us to "do logic." It could be, for example, that the only logically true sentences are the logically true identity sentences and their double denials.

We shall begin by considering the notion of *having the same form*, because this notion is involved in all the conditions we shall want to lay down. The difficulty is this: The sentences '$A \lor (B \lor \sim B)$' and '$A \lor C$' have in one sense the same form: they are both disjunctions. Yet one is a tautology and the other is not. If we insisted that they are not of the same *essential* form because there is not a component for component correspondence between them, then we should not be able—as we wish—to say that '$A \lor \sim A$' and '$(B \& C) \lor \sim (B \& C)$'

are of the same essential form. We may be able to get what we want by means of concepts of symmetrical and non-symmetrical iso-morphism. In the following exposition I shall frequently use the expression 'uniform replacement', which will mean that an expression is replaced in *all* of its occurrences by the same expression.

D24. S_i and S_j are *symmetrically isomorphic* in $St =_{df} S_i$ and S_j are both closed and there are one or more unitary designators and/or one or more variables of S_i such that if each of these designators is uniformly replaced by a designator of the same type and/or each of these variables is uniformly replaced by a variable of the same type, then S_j results; and conversely from S_j to S_i.

The "and conversely" clause guards against the possibility of a designator E_i being replaced in S_i by a designator E_j which already occurs in S_i and also against the possibility of altering the pattern of variables and quantifiers binding them.

Basically, the idea behind *non*-symmetrical isomorphism is this: you may start with a certain sentence S_i, and you may make certain replacements. But you may not touch the identity sign, the connectives, or the quantifiers. Further, parts of S_i may be "related" to other parts in such a way that if one part is replaced, then the other part calls for replacement by something "suitable." We shall require a few auxiliary definitions.

D25. S_i is an *instance* of S_j in $St =_{df} S_j$ is an open sentence of St and S_i is the result of uniformly replacing one or more free variables of S_j by different variables or constants of the same type as the variables replaced (and an instance will be open or closed accordingly as variables or constants are substituted).

D26. S_q and S_s are *related instances* in St of S_p and S_r respectively $=_{df} S_p$ and S_r are open sentences of St having one or more free variables in common and S_q is the result of uniformly replacing one or more of these common variables in S_p by constants or variables of the same type and S_s is the result of making the same replacement(s) in S_r (i.e., whatever replaces the variable v in S_p to yield S_q replaces v in S_r to yield S_s).

D27. S_i and S_j are *unrelated* in $St =_{df} S_i$ and S_j are not identical nor is one an instance of the other, and no component sentence of one of S_i and S_j is identical with a component sentence of the other or is an instance of a component sentence of the other.

D28. S_j is *non-symmetrically isomorphic* with S_i in St $=_{dt}$ one of the following conditions is satisfied:

(i) S_j is closed and is symmetrically isomorphic with S_i.

(ii) S_i is closed atomic and S_j is any closed sentence whatever.

(iii) S_i is open atomic and S_j is any open sentence whose free variables are all and only the free variables of S_i.

(iv) There are sentences S_k and S_l of St such that $S_i = \sim S_k$ and $S_j = \sim S_l$, and S_l is non-symmetrically isomorphic with S_k.

(v) There are sentences S_k, S_l, S_m and S_n of St and a binary connective B_1 of St such that $S_i = S_k B_1 S_l$ and $S_j = S_m B_1 S_n$, and

(a) S_k and S_l are unrelated, in which case S_m is non-symmetrically isomorphic with S_k and S_n is non-symmetrically isomorphic with S_l; *or*

(b) S_k and S_l are related in that

(α) there is a sentence which occurs in both S_k and S_l, in which case S_j is the result of uniformly replacing that sentence in S_i by a sentence non-symmetrically isomorphic with it; *or*

(β) there is an open sentence S_p which occurs in one of S_k and S_l and has an instance S_q occurring in the other, in which case S_j is the result of replacing S_p by an open sentence S_r non-symmetrically isomorphic with S_p, and S_q by an instance S_s of S_r such that S_q and S_s are related instances of S_p and S_r respectively; *or*

(c) S_k and S_l are related and there is a component sentence of one of S_k and S_l which is unrelated to any component sentence of the other and S_j is the result of uniformly replacing that sentence in S_i by a sentence non-symmetrically isomorphic with it.

(vi) S_i and S_j are both general sentences with the same initial quantifier, and the scope S_n of the initial quantifier of S_j is non-symmetrically isomorphic with the scope S_m of the initial quantifier of S_i.

(vii) S_j is non-symmetrically isomorphic with some sentence S_k which is non-symmetrically isomorphic with S_i.

The reader will notice that this is a rather stringent definition of non-symmetrical isomorphism—particularly in regard to open sentences. The reason is that we have a recursive definition intended to cover general sentences and if we did not exercise a fairly tight control in the early stages then we should have '$(x)(Qy)$' and '$(\exists y)[Py \lor (x)(Qy)]$' non-symmetrically isomorphic with '$(x)(Qx)$' and '$(\exists y)[Py \lor (x)(Qx)]$' respectively. And yet we shall want to say (as we at present cannot) that '$Px \supset Px$' is "of the same form" as '$Pa \supset Pa$' and '$Py \supset Py$'. And so we lay down the following definition:

D29. S_1 is *semi-isomorphic* with S_1 in $St =_{dt} S_1$ is a closed sentence of St containing one or more constants and S_j is the result of uniformly replacing one or more of those constants by variables of the same type; *or* S_1 is an open sentence containing one or more free variables and S_j is the result of uniformly replacing one or more of these variables by variables of the same type, provided that the replacing variable remains free; *or* S_j is non-symmetrically isomorphic with some sentence which is semi-isomorphic with S_1.

I shall assume without exhibition that it would be possible in the same way to define the three kinds of isomorphism for sentence sequences. This would enable us to say that if a given sequence is a derivation then any sequence either symmetrically, non-symmetrically, or semi-isomorphic with it is also a derivation.

Every sentence has associated with it a class of sentences which are symmetrically isomorphic with it (we shall call such a class a central class) and also an affiliated class of all and only those sentences which are non-symmetrically or semi-isomorphic with it. Let us call the sum of the central and the affiliated classes an isomorphism class. In virtue of D28(ii) and D29 the class of all the sentences of a language constitute an isomorphism class.

D30. K is an *isomorphism class* of sentences of $St =_{dt}$ there is a sentence S_1 of K such that any sentence S_j of St is a member of K if and only if S_j is non-symmetrically or semi-isomorphic with S_1.

D31. K_j is the *central class* of K_1 of $St =_{dt} K_1$ is an isomorphism class of sentences of St and K_j is a class of sentences of St such that S_1 is a member of K_j if and only if every sentence of K_1 is non-symmetrically or semi-isomorphic with S_1.

(It will be recalled that by D28(i) symmetrical isomorphism is a special case of non-symmetrical isomorphism.) We are now in a position to lay down the uniformity requirement.

R24. If a sentence S of St is logically true in St then every sentence of St non-symmetrically or semi-isomorphic with S is logically true in St.

By R24, if St is a language and K is an isomorphism class of sentences of St, then if the sentences of the central class of K are logically true then every sentence of K is logically true in St. In such a case we shall speak of a *logically true isomorphism class*. If *at least one member* of an isomorphism class is logically false we shall speak of a *logically false isomorphism class.*

Now we may consider ways and means of satisfying the second of the three general requirements mentioned earlier. We shall need, all told, three derivation concepts. Two will be required immediately.

D32. S_k is *directly derivable* in St from S_i and S_j $=_{df}$ the triple $(S_i;S_j;S_k)$ or the triple $(S_j;S_i;S_k)$ is a triple-member of the LP of St.

D33. S_n is *narrowly derivable* from S_i, S_j, . . ., S_m in St (or from the class $\{S_i,S_j, . . .,S_m\}$) $=_{df}$ there is a sequence Sq of sentences of St such that the last term of Sq is S_n and every other term of Sq is either identical with one of S_i, S_j, . . . , S_m or else is directly derivable from preceding terms of the sequence.

Having D32 we may now impose an obvious requirement.

R25. If S_i and S_j are logically true in St, and S_k is directly derivable from S_i and S_j in St, then S_k is logically true in St.

The following theorem is easily provable from R25 and D33.

T1. If St satisfies requirements R1–25, then, if K is a class of logically true sentences of St and S is narrowly derivable from K in St, S is logically true in St.

Narrow derivability is obviously a relation of not very general utility. Yet we can use it in imposing a very important requirement.

R26. There is a finite class κ of logically true isomorphism classes of St such that if K is the sum of the members of κ, then all logically true sentences of St (except Gödelian sentences) are narrowly derivable in St from a finite subclass of K. (It will be the business of the infinite mind mentioned on p. 70 to find such a finite class κ.)

This and subsequent allusions to Gödelian sentences are not strictly necessary since in this work we are not aiming at a general definition of language covering structures containing mathematics. The allusion is included to allow for the possibility of our definition being extended to cover such languages.

And now, finally, we may consider the matter of completeness (some kind of completeness, that is). It is the matter of ensuring that the class of logically true sentences is "sufficiently large". We might attempt to guarantee completeness by stipulating that every logical sentence (i.e., every sentence containing no designative expressions) shall be logically determinate. This seems to me to be too stringent a requirement. The sentence, 'There are at least two individuals' (or '$(\exists x)(\exists y)(x \neq y)$'), is a logical sentence but it follows from the *descriptively* analytic (or synthetic?) sentence '$a \neq b$' and would not be true unless there were as a matter of fact two distinct individuals. On this account I should prefer to regard '$(\exists x)(\exists y)(x \neq y)$' as merely descriptively analytic, notwithstanding the absence of descriptive expressions from it, and to get a completeness requirement that would not compel us to regard it as logically true. Oddly enough, the suggested requirement is in another sense too weak, for it does not, so far as I know, entail the condition to be laid down shortly (R28). We might require that every isomorphism class shall be logically true or logically false, but again this would compel us to regard '$(\exists x)(\exists y)(x \neq y)$' as logically true, contrary to the decision we have just made.

My intuitive understanding of completeness is this: every logical expression has a perfectly determinate meaning. That is to say, every sentence must have exhaustive truth and falsity conditions, every possible state of the world must make the sentence either true or false.[5] An intuitionistic language does not satisfy this kind of completeness requirement because in such a language the sentence '$\sim\sim A \supset A$' is not logically true but has no truth value in the case where 'A' is false. The task of ensuring completeness falls into three stages, the first having to do with the identity sign, the second with the connectives, and the third with the quantifiers. We shall need the third of our three derivation relations.

D34. S_n is *derivable* in St from S_1, S_j, . . ., S_m (or from the class $\{S_1, S_j, . . ., S_m\}$) $=_{df}$ there is a sequence Sq of sentences of St such that S_n is the last term of Sq and every other term of Sq is either identical with one of S_1, S_j, . . ., S_m, or is identical with a logically true sentence of St, or is directly derivable in St from preceding terms of Sq.

Theorem T2 is easily provable from R25, D34, and T1.

T2. If St satisfies requirements R1–26, then if K is a class of logically true sentences of St, and S is derivable in St from K, S is logically true in St.

It will be noted that by reason of the appearance of 'logically true sentence' in D34 instead of, as is usual, 'axiom', we have a rather

---

[5]It may be that in the case of subjunctive conditionals this would be too strong a requirement. However, we shall not get started on *that*.

trivial relation. But we can now indirectly guarantee a "sufficiently large" class of logically true sentences by insisting that certain derivations shall be possible. It does not matter that these derivations are trivial. Again we shall proceed by first getting the identity sign out of the way.

R27. If $E_i = E_j$ is a sentence of St and if S_i contains E_i and S_j is the result of replacing E_i in one, some, or all of its occurrences in S_i by E_j, then S_j is derivable from $E_i = E_j$ and S_i.

The connectives will cause us more trouble.

D35. S is a *purely molecular sentence* of St $=_{df}$ S is a closed molecular sentence of St all of whose ultimate sentential components are atomic.

D36. K is a *base class* of S in St $=_{df}$ S is a purely molecular sentence of St and if S_i is an ultimate sentential component of S (and therefore atomic) then either S_i or $\sim S_i$, but not both, is a member of K.

R28. If S is a purely molecular sentence of St and K is a base class of S, then either S is derivable from K or else $\sim S$ is derivable from K.

A base class of a purely molecular sentence S corresponds to a line in the truth table of S and R28 corresponds to a requirement that a molecular sentence shall have a truth value for every combination of truth values of its ultimate components. Thus we guarantee that our languages satisfy our intuitive completeness requirement *in regard to their sentential logic*. With one more requirement we can prove three theorems.

R29. If S is derivable in St from $K + \{S_i\}$ and from $K + \{\sim S_i\}$ then S is derivable in St from K.

T3. If St satisfies R1–29 and if S is a purely molecular sentence of St which is derivable in St from every one of its base classes, then S is logically true in St.

Proof: Let the distinct atomic components of S be

$$S_{i_1}, S_{i_2}, \ldots, S_{i_n}$$

and let the members of any base class be

$$S_{p_1}, S_{p_2}, \ldots, S_{p_n},$$

where

$$S_{p_k} = S_{i_k}$$

or

$$S_{p_k} = {\sim} S_{i_k} \ (k = 1 \text{ to } n).$$

S is derivable from any base class

$$\{S_{i_1}, S_{p_2}, \ldots, S_{p_n}\}$$

and from any base class

$${\sim} S_{i_1}, S_{p_2}, \ldots, S_{p_n}\}.$$

Hence (from R29) S is derivable from any partial base class

$$\{S_{p_2}, \ldots, S_{p_n}\}.$$

And if S is derivable from any partial base class

$$\{S_{i_k}, S_{p_{k+1}}, \ldots, S_{p_n}\}$$

and from any partial base class

$${\sim} S_{i_k}, S_{p_{k+1}}, \ldots, S_{p_n}\} \ (k = 1 \text{ to } n),$$

then S is derivable from any partial base class

$$\{S_{p_{k+1}}, \ldots, S_{p_n}\}.$$

Hence, by induction on k, S is derivable from any partial base class

$$\{S_{p_n}\}$$

that is, from

$$S_{i_n}$$

and from

$${\sim} S_{i_n}.$$

Hence if S_r is any logically true sentence of St, S is derivable from

$$\{S_{i_n}, S_r\}$$

and from

$${\sim} S_{i_n}, S_r\}.$$

Hence (from R29) S is derivable from S_r and (from T2) is logically true in St.

T4. If St satisfies requirements R1–29, then if a purely molecular sentence S is derivable in St from at least one of its base classes, there is at least one logically true sentence of St non-symmetrically isomorphic with S in St.

Let the atomic components of S be

$$S_{i_1}, S_{i_2}, \ldots, S_{i_n}.$$

Let K_p be a base class

$$\{S_{p_1}, S_{p_2}, \ldots, S_{p_n}\}$$

from which S is derivable, where

$$S_{p_k} = S_{i_k}$$

or

$$S_{p_k} = {\sim}S_{i_k} \quad (k = 1 \text{ to } n).$$

Let S_r be a logically true identity sentence and let K_q be a class

$$\{S_{q_1}, S_{q_2}, \ldots, S_{q_n}\},$$

such that

$$S_{q_k} = S_r$$

if

$$S_{p_k} = S_{i_k}$$

and

$$S_{q_k} = {\sim}{\sim}S_r$$

if

$$S_{p_k} = {\sim}S_{i_k}.$$

From D21 and R21 ${\sim}{\sim}S_r$ is logically true and hence the class K_q is logically true. Let S_1 be the sentence obtained from S by uniformly replacing

$$S_{i_k}$$

in S by S_r if

$$S_{p_k} = S_{i_k}$$

and by ${\sim}S_r$ if

$$S_{p_k} = {\sim}S_{i_k}.$$

The sentence S_1 is non-symmetrically isomorphic with S. S is derivable from K_p and to the derivation of S from K_p there will be a non-symmetrically isomorphic sequence which is a derivation of S_1 from K_q. Since K_q is logically true, then (from T2) S_1 is logically true in *St*.

T5. If *St* satisfies requirements R1–29 then every isomorphism class of *St* whose central class contains purely molecular sentences is either logically true in *St* or logically false in *St*.

For either a purely molecular sentence S of *St* is derivable from every one of its base classes, in which case (from T3) it is logically true in *St* and (from R24) every sentence non-symmetrically or semi-isomorphic with it is logically true. Or $\sim S$ is derivable from at least one of its base classes, in which case (from T4) there is a sentence S_1 such that $\sim S_1$ is non-symmetrically isomorphic with $\sim S$ and is logically true. Then S_1 is logically false (D21) and is non-symmetrically isomorphic with S (D28(iv)). Hence the theorem.

In T4 and, by implication, T5, use was made of an unspecified logically true identity sentence. If we had stipulated that there is at least one logically true purely molecular sentence, it would not have been necessary to invoke an identity sentence. In that case T5 would, in effect, have been a proof of completeness for the sentential logic of structures satisfying R1–29.

We may now turn our attention to the quantifiers of structures which are to be languages. Suppose we have a structure satisfying requirements R1–29 and containing just the individual constants '*a*', '*b*' and '*c*'. (By R2 every language has only a finite number of individual constants.) Let us define *partial* quantifiers, symbolizing them with square brackets.

$$[x] \ldots x \ldots =_{\text{df}} \ldots a \ldots \& \ldots b \ldots \& \ldots c \ldots .$$
$$[\exists x] \ldots x \ldots =_{\text{df}} \ldots a \ldots \vee \ldots b \ldots \vee \ldots c \ldots .$$

The foregoing are schemata: any individual variable may be substituted in the definition. If the structure in question happens to lack signs of conjunction and disjunction, then in place of a conjunction '$A \& B$' we should have to use '$\sim(A \supset \sim B)$' and in place of a disjunction '$A \vee B$' we should have to use '$\sim A \supset B$'. Now the logic of partial quantification will be part of sentential logic. We can extend the idea of a base class to cover sentences with partial quantification. If S_1 is a partially quantified sentence the scope of whose partial quantifier is an open atomic sentence S_v, then a base class of

S_1 comprises just one of the instantiation of S_v for 'a' and its negation, just one of the instantiation of S_v for 'b' and its negation, and just one of the instantiation of S_v for 'c' and its negation. Clearly the notion of a base class can be extended to cover more complicated cases, for example, where the scope of the partial quantifier is logically complex and where the partially quantified sentence is a component of a larger sentence. It will follow from R28 that for any base class K of a sentence S containing a partial quantifier, S is derivable from K or $\sim S$ is derivable from K. All the foregoing remarks may be generalized to cover partial quantifiers of any type.

We might now require that if a sentence with a partial quantifier is logically true then the result of replacing that quantifier with the corresponding genuine quantifier is also logically true. This is too strong, because we should have '$[\exists x](Px) \supset (Pa \vee Pb \vee Pc)$' as logically true but we do not want '$(\exists x)(Px) \supset (Pa \vee Pb \vee Pc)$' to be logically true. And so we impose a weaker requirement. If a sentence with partial quantification is logically true and contains no closed instances of the scope of the partial quantifier elsewhere in the sentence, then the result of replacing the partial quantifier by a genuine quantifier is logically true. This would presumably guarantee that we should have as logically true sentences like '$(x)(Px \supset Qx) \supset [(\exists x)(Px) \supset (\exists x)(Qx)]$' and the forms of de Morgan's Theorem for quantifiers, '$\sim(x)(Px) \equiv (\exists x)(\sim Px)$', etc. Also it would give us as logically true '$(\exists x)(\sim Qa \,\&\, Px) \supset [\sim Qa \,\&\, (\exists x)(Px)]$', which in turn, via the uniformity requirement R24, would give us '$(\exists x)(\sim Pa \,\&\, Px) \supset [\sim Pa \,\&\, (\exists x)(Px)]$'. We want both of these to be logically true in spite of the fact that the second one contains a closed instance of the scope of one of the quantifiers. Thus we guarantee that there shall be rules for importing and exporting quantifiers.

And now we may attempt to elaborate the foregoing more exactly. Earlier (R18) we stipulated that the quantifiers are of two main kinds, each quantifier containing, in addition to a variable, the common mark of its kind. We are using 'Q' as a doubly varying variable, ranging over the quantifiers of St, 'Q_v' as a trebly varying variable ranging over the quantifiers of St having 'v' as their variable, and 'S_v' as a trebly varying variable ranging over the open sentences of St containing a free occurrence of v.

R30. There is a quantifier Q_v of St such that every instance of S_v is derivable in St from $Q_v S_v$ and if S is closed then S is derivable in St from $Q_v S$.

R31. Every quantifier Q_v of St of the same kind (i.e., having the same mark) as the quantifier mentioned in R30 has the same property, namely, that every instance of S_v is derivable in St from Q_vS_v and if S is closed then S is derivable in St from Q_vS.

D37. E is a *universal quantifier* of St $=_{df}$ E is a quantifier having the property mentioned in R31.

D38. E is an *existential quantifier* of St $=_{df}$ E is a quantifier but is not a universal quantifier.

We may now use '(v)' and '$(\exists v)$' as restricted variables ranging respectively over the universal and existential quantifiers of St containing the variable v. The following requirements are self-explanatory.

R32. The sentence $(\exists v)S_v$ is derivable in St from every instance of S_v.

R33. If the sentence $(v)S_v$ is not logically true, it is not derivable from any class of instances of S_v.

The following can be proved easily:

T6. If St satisfies R1–33 and contains a sign of disjunction, then no disjunction of instances of S_v is derivable from $(\exists v)S_v$ unless it is logically true in St.

R34. Let St_1 be a structure satisfying requirements R1–33 and let St_j be a structure obtained from St_1 by the substitution of a partial quantifier (as earlier explained) for every genuine quantifier of St_1. If S_j is a logically true sentence of St_j containing one or more partial quantifiers $Q_1, Q_j, \ldots$, but containing no closed instances of the scopes of those partial quantifiers, and if S_1 is the result of replacing all the partial quantifiers of S_j by their corresponding genuine quantifiers in St_1, then S_1 is logically true in St_1.

One final requirement:

R35. If every instance of S_v is logically true in St, then $(v)S_v$ is logically true in St. (That is, true Gödelian sentences are logically true.)

And, at last, our *terminus ad quem*:

D39. St is a language $=_{df}$ St satisfies requirements R1–35.

We may also define 'proper sub-language':

D40. St_j is a *proper sub-language* of $St_1 =_{dt} St_j$ and St_1 are both languages and the LP of St_j is a proper sub-class of the LP of St_1. (If the
DP of St_j were a proper sub-class of the DP of St_1 then necessarily
the LP of St_j would be a proper subclass of the LP of St_1 anyway.)

§23. 'TRUE'

Having arrived at a definition of 'language' we may now use the
variables 'L', 'L_1', 'L_j', etc. as restricted variables ranging over all
and only languages. We may assume that in the key definitions of
earlier sections 'St' has been replaced by 'L'. We may now make a first
attempt at defining 'true'.

D41. S is *atomically true* in $L =_{dt} S$ is an atomic sentence of L and
there is a proposition p such that S G-designates p in L and p.

D42. S is a *true identity sentence* of $L =_{dt} S$ is an identity sentence of
L with designative arguments and these arguments G-designate in L
the same entity.

D43. S is *basically true* in $L =_{dt} S$ is a true identity sentence of L
or S is atomically true in L or there is a sentence S_1 of L such that S_1
is an atomic sentence of L or an identity sentence of L, $S = \sim S_1$,
and S_1 is not true in L.

D44'. S is *true* in $L =_{dt} S$ is basically true in L, or S is derivable in
L from a class of true sentences of L, or every sentence which is derivable in L from S or derivable in L from S together with other true
sentences of L, is true in L.

It will be recalled that every sentence is either atomic, identity,
molecular, or general. Our definition of 'true' fits purely molecular
sentences: A sentence which is syntactically a negation will be true
if and only if the sentential component is not true, a sentence which is
syntactically a conjunction will be true if and only if both components
are true, and a disjunction will be true if and only if either component
is true. But we run into trouble with general sentences. Suppose our
language has names for just the individuals a, b, and c, and that they
all have the property P but that some other unnamed individual lacks
the property P. Then, although we should wish to call '$(x)(Px)$' false,
this sentence has no false *non-general* derivates in the language—
'Pa', 'Pb', and 'Pc' all being true. And similarly for existentially
quantified sentences. There might be such a sentence, which, although

we should wish to call it true, is not derivable from any true non-general sentences of the language. However, we note that every entity is named in some language or other. What we want is a definition of 'translation' by which we can both restrict and relax D44' in the desired directions.

D45. E_j of L_j is a *simple translation* of E_i of L_i $=_{dt}$ one of the following conditions is satisfied:

(i) E_i and E_j are both designative in L_i and L_j respectively, and G-designate the same entity in L_i and L_j respectively.

(ii) E_i and E_j are both variables of L_i and L_j respectively and are of the same type in L_i and L_j respectively.

(iii) E_i is the identity sign (the implication sign, the negation sign) of L_i and E_j is the identity sign (the implication sign, the negation sign) of L_j.

D46. The binary connectives B_m, B_n, . . . of L_j are respective translations of the binary connectives B_i, B_j, . . . of L_i $=_{dt}$ for every S_i of L_i and for every S_j of L_j, if S_i is a logically true purely molecular sentence of L_i containing only designators which have simple translations into L_j, and S_j is the result of replacing each designator of S_i, by its translation into L_j and of replacing the implication and negation signs in S_i (supposing either or both occur in S_i) by the implication and negation signs respectively of L_j and of replacing B_i by B_m, B_j by B_n, etc., then S_j is logically true in L_j.

D47. S_j of L_j is a *translation* of S_i of L_i $=_{dt}$ one of the following conditions is satisfied:

(i) S_i and S_j are both atomic sentences or both identity sentences (open or closed) of L_i and L_j respectively and the nth unitary component of S_j is a simple translation of the nth unitary component of S_i, provided that if v_i occurs in the nth place in S_i and v_j occurs in the nth place in S_j, then for every place at which v_i occurs in S_i, v_j occurs in S_j, and conversely.

(ii) S_i and S_j are both molecular (open or closed) in L_i and L_j respectively and S_j is the result of replacing the connectives of S_i by their translations into L_j and of replacing the ultimate sentential components of S_i by translations into L_j, provided that . . . as in (i).

(iii) S_i and S_j are both general in L_i and L_j respectively, the initial quantifier Q_i of S_i and the initial quantifier Q_j of S_j are of the same kind (universal or existential), the scope of Q_j is a translation of the scope of Q_i and if the variable v_i of the quantifier Q_i occurs in the nth place of S_i then the variable v_j of Q_j occurs in the nth place of S_j, and conversely.

(iv) There is a language L_k and a sentence S_k of L_k such that S_k of L_k is a translation of S_i of L_i and S_j of L_j is a translation of S_k of L_k.

We may now formulate a definition of truth.

D48. S is *true* in L $=_{df}$
  A. S is closed and one of the following conditions is satisfied:
    (i) S is basically true in L.
    (ii) S is molecular but is not the negation of an atomic or identity sentence, and S is derivable in L from a class of true sentences of L.
    (iii) S is an existentially quantified sentence and is derivable from a true sentence of L *or* there is an L_i and an S_i of L_i such that S_i is true in L_i and S in L is a translation of S_i of L_i.
    (iv) S is a universally quantified sentence and every sentence derivable in L from S is true *and* for every L_i and for every S_i of L_i, if S_i in L_i is a translation of S of L then S_i is true in L_i.
  or B. S is open, contains a free occurrence of v, and $(v)S$ is true in L.

The difficulty noted earlier is now overcome. For if there is some individual which lacks the property P there is some language containing a name for that individual. The atomic sentence ascribing that property to that individual will not be true in that language and hence the translation into that language of '$(x)(Px)$' will not be true and '$(x)(Px)$' will not be true in our original language. We may offer one more definition and a theorem before continuing.

D49. S is *false* in L $=_{df}$ S is not true in L.

T7. Every logically true sentence of L is true (since a logically true sentence is derivable from any sentence and *a fortiori* from any true sentence).

There is a quite fundamental matter which calls for attention here. It concerns the fact that with the present method semantics and syntax are much more closely wedded than they are for, say, Carnap. Where Carnap has separate syntactical and semantical concepts of necessary truth (C-truth and L-truth) we have only one, logical truth. And it is handled by methods which, if not strictly syntactical (in the sense of "in total abstraction from meaning"), are nevertheless closer to traditional syntax than to semantics. And 'true' is defined with the help of the syntactical concept of *derivability*. (This procedure reflects our pre-analytic intuitions, because we should ordinarily say that derivations must lead from truths to truths and not from truths to falsehoods.) By reason of the latter fact, questions concerning the possibility of non-normal interpretations of object languages simply do not arise. In his *Formalization* (p. 140), Carnap is concerned about the possibility of '$(x)(Px)$' having a non-normal interpretation whereby it would mean, "every individual is P and b is Q." That is to say, in interpreting the calculus containing '$(x)(Px)$' one might have the truth condition: '$(x)(Px)$' is true if and only if every individual is P and b is Q. But with the present method (in particular, D48) this could only be a truth condition of '$(x)(Px)$' if 'Qb' were derivable from '$(x)(Px)$'. Since the deduction theorem is presumably true of our languages we should then have '$(x)(Px) \supset Qb$' as logically true in the language. By the uniformity requirement R24, we should have every sentence of the same form logically true, including '$(x)(x = x) \supset (b \neq b)$' which is, in fact, self-contradictory. But by the consistency requirement R22, this is impossible. Thus the uniformity requirement and the consistency requirement, together with the intimate way in which truth and derivability are connected, preserve us against the possibility of sentences of our languages having the kind of non-normal truth-conditions under discussion, where truth is defined by D48.

Now it is merely a feature, not necessarily a merit, of the present method that the difficulty of non-normal interpretations does not arise. (But it can be a defect of a method that it generates difficulties *gratuitously*.) However, when we consider not just the object languages of G, but the total system, including object languages and the meta-language, we get the problem of non-normal interpretations at a higher level.

Suppose we have a language defined in the manner employed in chapter III, §8. But we misinterpret it as follows:

For S (a full sentence, not a component) we understand 'not-S'	
For '$\sim$'	we understand 'not'
For '$=$'	'$\neq$'
For '&'	'or'
For '$\vee$'	'and'
For '$(x)(Px)$'	'for some x, Px'
For '$(\exists x)(Px)$'	'for all x, Px'
For '$A \supset B$'	'not (not-A and B)'
(i.e., '$\sim A \vee B$')	(i.e., 'if B then A')

In the last case, it is only full conditionals that may be so interpreted. Conditionals as parts of full sentences must be expanded and (mis-) interpreted according to the rules governing the expansion. It might be noted that the non-normal interpretation given here is exactly equivalent to misinterpreting every atomic sentence (but not an identity sentence) as its own denial. We shall give some examples, showing how logical truths go into logical truths and derivations go into derivations.

A & *B*	Not (*A* or *B*)
∴*A*	∴Not *A*

A	Not *A*
B	Not *B*
∴*A* & *B*	∴Not (*A* or *B*)

A	Not *A*
∴*A* ∨ *B*	∴Not(*A* & *B*)

(*A* & *B*) ⊃ *A*	If *A* then (*A* or *B*)

$A \supset [B \supset (A \ \& \ B)]$
i.e., $\sim A \ \lor \ \sim B \ \lor \ (A \ \& \ B)$

Not{Not *A* and [Not *B* and (*A* or *B*)]}

∼*A*	Not Not *A*
A ∨ *B*	Not (*A* and *B*)
∴*B*	∴Not *B*

a = *a*	Not (*a* ≠ *a*)

Pa	Not *Pa*
∴(∃*x*)(*Px*)	∴Not for all *x*, *Px*

(*x*)(*Px*)	Not there is some *x* such that *Px*
∴*Pa*	∴Not *Pa*

Now if we apply D48 to our misinterpretation it turns out that we have merely defined a concept which is different from the usual concept of truth. The sentence '*Pa*' alone means that it is not the case that *a* is *P* (i.e., is true if and only if *a* is not *P*) but is "D48-true" if and only if *a* is *P*. And the sentence '*Pa* & *Qb*', which is syntactically a conjunction, means that (is true if and only if) it is not the case that a is P or b is Q. Yet it is D48-true if and only if a is P and b is Q. Thus we see the possibility of a non-normal interpretation of the total system. It is the case that the non-normal interpretation of the object language is not such as to preserve the truth values of sentences from the normal to the non-normal interpretation. But that is neither here nor there. The important thing is that logical truth and the derivability relations are maintained. Thus the logical signs have the same "formal" meaning but different interpretations. The difficulty here, if indeed it is a difficulty, still confronts Carnap, so far as I can see, even after he has completed the *Formalization of Logic*.

My own view is that the lacuna or lack of completeness indicated is due simply to the fact that we are doing semantics and not pragmatics. And rather than go to heroic lengths in an attempt to rectify the situation at this stage, I should prefer to postpone the matter. After all, we shall want to do pragmatics eventually. All that is necessary is that in defining 'S G-designates p for person P' we shall have a definition which will entail that if S G-designates p for P, then P interprets S to mean p (to be true if and only if p) and does not interpret it to mean not-p. This will be sufficient to guarantee that a sentence is D48-true for P if and only if it is true for P in the ordinary pre-analytic sense.

§24. GENERAL REMARKS

We may pause now to consider some of the objections to the foregoing definition of 'language'. It must be conceded that although the definition covers an infinity of languages, it is nevertheless exceedingly narrow in scope. It is confined to symbolic languages and, moreover, to a class of symbolic languages which are typographically of a special sort. The sentences of our languages all have a linear order of signs. It is assumed also that all the languages employ the same system of punctuation, whatever that system may be. It might be worth noting that we could have introduced simple licences to enable our definition to cover two-valued extensional languages and nominalistic languages. In an extensional language we should have the sign of identity occurring *only* with individual expressions and in a nominalistic language we should have, in addition, only quantifiers containing individual variables. Nevertheless, some types of symbolic languages are not covered by our definition, intuitionistic and modal systems, for example. And our definition does not even come close to covering languages of the type of used languages. Actually, the framing of a *technically adequate* and *fully general* definition of language would be an impossibly difficult undertaking, and perhaps even unprofitable. Yet the narrowness of the allegedly general definition of language we have finally arrived at does arouse an uneasy suspicion that the present undertaking is trivial. This is a question which will be taken up below (p. 130).

Two other shortcomings might be mentioned. Languages as defined by D39 do not contain mathematics. We might have introduced a licence to the effect that *St* may contain a mathematical superstructure, but then we should require a general definition of 'mathematical superstructure'. No such general definition will be given but in the Appendix we shall give an example of a specific mathematical superstructure. The other shortcoming has to do with the fact that D39 covers only languages in primitive notation. What is envisaged in the way of a definitional superstructure is this: we lay a third term beside the DP and LP of a language (so that a language would be a triple and not a couple). The third term, or definitional superstructure, would be a class of couples, the terms of the couples being sentences of the language in question, the first term being a sentence with a definiendum expression, the second being its expansion. Obviously we should not want to regard any class of couples of sentences as being a definitional superstructure, and so we should have the task of finding a suitable set of requirements to be satisfied by a definitional superstructure. That might prove to be a fairly large undertaking.

There is another objection to the present definition of language—the complaint that the definition is counter-intuitive (which, in a sense, it is). It will be pointed out that on the present account the city of Chicago is part of, or, in Nelson Goodman's phrase, an ultimate factor of, any language in which it is G-designated. And yet we should normally say that Chicago is extra-linguistic. Thus the concept herein defined may be a very fine concept, but it is not the concept of language.

I may say at once that I am not quite clear as to what kind of force a charge of counter-intuitiveness is supposed to have. The method employed in this book would be described as the method of fabricating certain entities out of other entities in such a way that the fabricated entities shall satisfy antecedently intuited identity conditions. I do not think that the definition of 'language' offered here is markedly more counter-intuitive than the definition of positive and negative integers as equivalence classes of couples of natural numbers, or Whitehead's definition of points as nested volumes. In short, the method employed here must be at least fifty years old and should raise no eyebrows at this late date. In connection with the so-called extra-linguistic status of Chicago, it seems to me that in describing Chicago as extra-linguistic we intended to say only that you cannot put the city of Chicago on the printed page. Chicago is outside the vocabulary. Nobody, least of all myself, would wish to deny this. But if it is charged that D39 *wrongly* incorporates Chicago into the English language and makes it no longer extra-linguistic, then a suspicion arises that the complaint issues out of the mistake of identifying a language with its vocabulary. Surely the opposition would not wish to maintain that you can define the English language without reference to Chicago. What I have been doing in this study is to make it clear how this reference might be made.

Moreover, it seems likely that our pre-analytic concepts of *language-hood* and *use of a language* are so tangled up together that any attempt to untangle them will produce results having an appearance of paradox. In any case, in laying down the criteria of adequacy, C2, C3, and C4, we were guided by our pre-analytic concept of language. Assuming the usual identity conditions for classes and sequences then our definition does conform to the original criteria of adequacy. Surely, therefore, we have done our duty by the pre-analytic concept.

Not quite. And it is the margin of failure here which is responsible for the counter-intuitiveness of the present account. When we return to the problem of teaching Hermann L_1, we find that even after we have stated in German the composition of L_1, Hermann can neither speak it nor understand it. Again it may be necessary to assume that Hermann is a bit dull, but that is a legitimate heuristic assumption. The point is that to tell a person that L_1 is a couple of such and such a character is not to tell him how to use L_1. Our account of language does not satisfy convention C1 (above, p. 16). We may conclude that there is still work to do. After clearing away other matters in chapter VI we shall be ready in chapter VII to outline a programme. I am not conceding that D39 is in any sense wrong or misguided. I am conceding that it does not give us a full explication of the concept of *languagehood*.

VI. PROTO-FACTS

§25. EXISTENCE ASSUMPTIONS, CONTINGENT SIGNIFICANCE, AND
DESCRIPTIVE INCOMPLETENESS[1]

In this chapter I shall want to justify some of the more debatable procedures in chapters III and V, especially the recognition of G-propositions. What we shall do is forget about what has gone before and start in afresh on a problem that has not even been mentioned yet: the problem of existence assumptions. Russell states the problem nicely in his *Math. Phil.*, p. 203n: "The primitive propositions of *Principia Mathematica* are such as to allow the inference that at least one individual exists. But I now view this as a defect in logical purity." Like most logistic systems, *PM* contains sentences like '$(\exists x)(Fx \lor \sim Fx)$' and '$(\exists x)(x = x)$' as theorems, and as such, they presumably are necessarily true. Yet they say that there exists at least one individual and we should normally regard it as a contingent fact that there exist any concrete individuals at all. It is on this account that Russell is uneasy about his existentially quantified theorems.

The point at issue has been extensively discussed. Quine, in reviewing one of these discussions, writes, ". . . familiar logic accepts '$(\exists x)(fx \lor \sim fx)$' as a theorem and in such ways frankly asserts that there are entities. But Nelson and others begrudge logic this minimum ontological content . . . ."[2] But the point is this: we shall certainly boggle at a procedure by which there occur as theorems statements which would have been false had the facts been different from what they are. If there were no individuals—an apparently conceivable state of affairs—then these existentially quantified theorems would not be true. What I shall suggest is that these theorems are necessarily true if significant at all, *but are only contingently significant.*

Let us suppose that, without too many preconceptions about the word 'signifies', we are prepared to say things like

(1)   'Chicago' signifies Chicago (in English, always),
(2)   'large' signifies Large.[3]

Apart from a few additions, subtractions, and alterations, this section is substantially a reproduction of the contents of my paper, *Existence*.

[2]W. V. Quine, *Rev. Nelson*, p. 54.

[3]In *Existence* I used the word 'means'. I now believe it will be safer to keep away from that word.

Now it might be objected that (2) suggests that 'signifies' is synonymous with 'means' or 'has as its sense', in which case 'signifies' is inappropriate in (1). For Chicago is the nominatum or designatum of 'Chicago', not its sense or its meaning. Nevertheless there is this circumstance to be considered: if you do not know what 'Chicago' designates, then you could not set about verifying the sentence 'Chicago is large'.[4] And if you do not know how to verify the sentence 'Chicago is large', then, according to received doctrines, you do not know the significance of the sentence. And if you do not know the significance of the sentence it must be because you do not know the significance of one of the components. And since you know the significance of 'large', it must be because you do not know the significance of 'Chicago'. Thus failure to know the designatum of 'Chicago' is the same as failure to know its significance and we are justified in taking the *significance* of an individual constant to be its designatum.

The foregoing argument is somewhat casual but it will serve to provide a rough sort of rationale for the use of the words 'signifies' and 'non-significant'. Naturally I want 'non-significant' to be read as 'meaningless', or at least read with most of the pejorative connotations of the latter word, even though systematically, *non-significance* and *meaninglessness* are not quite the same. Their difference comes out in connection with words like 'Pegasus' and 'Cerberus', which, since they do not signify *anything*, are strictly non-significant.[5] Yet it will be insisted that these words are meaningful and a question raised as to whether *non-significance* is of any interest as a substitute for *meaninglessness*. I shall simply have to ask the reader to be patient at this point and I shall do my best to pick up Pegasus and Cerberus later.

Now back to the problem of existence assumptions. The present approach owes a great deal to F. P. Ramsey. I shall simply draw attention to two of his statements (*Foundations*, p. 60):

But suppose there were no individuals, and therefore no values of x, then the above formula ['$(\exists x) . x = x$'] is absolute nonsense . . . . 'There are at least n individuals' is always a tautology or a contradiction, never a genuine proposition. We cannot, therefore, say anything about the number of individuals, since, when we attempt to do so we never succeed in constructing a genuine proposition, but only a formula which is either tautological or self-contradictory. The number of individuals can, in Wittgenstein's phrase, only be shown, and it will be shown by whether the above formulae are tautological or contradictory.

---

[4]See above, p. 46.

[5]But we should maintain, as we did in chapter III, that descriptions, although significant, do not get their significance by signifying any*thing*. The point is that 'Cerberus' and 'Pegasus', unlike descriptions, are syntactically of the class of words (*viz.*, names) which, if they are significant, are significant by signifying some*thing*.

Presumably Ramsey means that the sentence, 'There are precisely four individuals', is a tautology or contradiction *depending upon the state of the world*. The implication (and this is what is useful to us) seems to be that if *as a matter of fact* there are precisely four individuals, then *necessarily* ('$\supset \square$', *not* ' $\mapsto$ ') there are precisely four individuals. The oddity of this result is worth remarking.

I am not presenting Ramsey's views in detail because he is doing propositional logic whereas I prefer to do the analysis in terms of sentences. And I do not wish to subscribe to the Wittgenstein-Ramsey interpretation of quantification, on which general propositions are taken as conjunctions or disjunctions. To make matters simple I shall assume that existentially quantified theorems are derived from universally quantified theorems via singular theorems. Logicians would normally find the following argument unexceptionable:

$$(x)(x = x)$$
$$a = a$$
$$\therefore (\exists x)(x = x).$$

In the argument the first sentence is an already proven theorem and 'a' an individual constant, the second step being derived from the first by instantiation, the third from the second by existential generalization. Thus, with the foregoing stipulation regarding the derivation of existentially quantified theorems, the occurrence of such theorems depends upon the presence in the language of individual constants.

And so let us glance at these constants, and in particular, at the sentence '$a = b$'. (*Cf.* 'Tully = Cicero'.) Wittgenstein has asked (*Tractatus*, 4.243), "Can we understand two names without knowing whether they signify the same thing or two different things? Can we understand a proposition in which two names occur, without knowing if they mean the same or different things?" Even if we substitute 'sentence' for 'proposition' in this question the answer would presumably be in the negative. We may say then, that '$a = b$', if true, is analytic, in the sense that one who knows the significance of 'a' and of 'b' (knows what they designate) will know that '$a = b$' is true. If he knows what the constants signify he need make no further appeal to fact in order to know that the sentence is true. But we cannot say that '$a = b$' is analytic in the sense of being true no matter what. For if there were no world of individuals, 'a' and 'b' would lack significance and '$a = b$' would likewise be non-significant. We shall say, therefore, that the sentence in question is necessarily true (analytic) but *contingently significant.*[6] The world could have differed so as to render the statement non-significant, but it could not have differed so as to render it false. For the same reason '$a = a$' is necessarily true and contingently significant. In this latter case the sentence is not merely analytic but is logically true.

We might choose to regard '$(\exists x)(x = x)$' as necessarily significant and contingently provable—the existence of a proof being contingent on the existence of significant individual constants, which in turn is contingent on the existence of individuals. By this procedure we should have provided our system with an *a priori* guarantee that false statements would not be provable. But on this view the status of existentially quantified theorems would seem to be so anomalous that it would be preferable to regard them as contingently significant. This can be given effect by the following general convention: a variable is significant if and only if its range is non-empty. If there were no individuals, then 'x' would be non-significant, and also '$(\exists x)(x = x)$'.

With a clear conscience we may now grant logic the "minimum ontological content" Quine asks for. For an assumption or presupposition of existence to which the logician commits himself is not such as to cause any falsifiable statements to appear as theorems of his system. These existentially quantified theorems are necessarily true, they could not possibly be false. But they are contingently significant. The facts might have been such as to deprive them of their significance. And we see that what Russell regards as a defect in *PM* is not a defect at all (as would be the occurrence of a falsifiable theorem) but, rather, simply a curiosity.

We now have the following result: If there were no concrete world (= if there were no individuals) then there would be no ordinary-type languages (what will be called *name-languages*, that is, languages containing individual constants) in which it would be possible to record this lamentable fact. The sentence '$\sim(\exists x)(x = x)$' is necessarily false in such a language, it does not refer to a possible state of affairs.

But let us consider a second type of language, in which names of individuals are replaced by definite descriptions. Such languages will be called 'description-languages'. A description, '$(\imath x)(Px)$' would function in inferences of instantiation only with an additional factual premise, '$E!(\imath x)(Px)$'. In other words, instead of the theorem '$(x)(Qx) \supset Qa$' we should have

$$(x)(Qx) \supset [E!(\imath x)(Px) \supset Q(\imath x)(Px)].$$

With this procedure, no existentially quantified sentence would occur

[6]The notion of contingent significance comes to me from Rulon Wells.

as a theorem and our language would be guaranteed against the occurrence of falsifiable theorems, even if we did not stipulate that the significance of individual variables is dependent upon their range being non-empty. The sentences '$(\exists x)(x = x)$' and '$\sim(\exists x)(x = x)$' would both be synthetic, the latter expressing the possibility of there being no individuals.

In order to find out what is wrong with this proposal we shall have to open up the *ante rem–in re* question. In one sense, properties, if they exist at all, exist *ante rem*. If we wish to say that Red exists, we should write '$(\exists F)(F = \text{Red})$'. This is a provable statement, in no way contingent upon the truth of '$(\exists x)(\text{Red}(x))$' ("Something is red"). All that is required is that 'Red' should be significant. And even if Red is unexemplified, the word 'red' would gain its significance from occurring in true sentences like 'Red is between orange and purple', 'Red is complementary to green'. But when we examine the significance conditions of 'red' we find that in a different sense, Red exists *in re*.

Suppose that the statement, 'Everything is red', were true. But in such a case 'red' would be deprived of its distinctive significance. If 'red' were taken as signifying a specific shade then presumably we should have different kinds of experience according as our eyes were open or shut, but apart from that, the sense of sight would provide us with no information about the world. If Red were a hue, then (supposing the truth of 'Everything is red') vision would give us the kind of information provided by a black and white photograph. But we should not comprehend what is meant by the statement, 'Everything is red and not green'. Thus the statement, 'Everything is red', does not describe a possible state of affairs. Yet we shrink from describing it as necessarily false, and its denial, 'Something is not red', as necessarily true. It seems to have a somewhat anomalous status of its own. (The foregoing example is not really necessary to exhibit the sense in which properties exist *in re*, but I shall make use of it shortly.)

Now suppose that there were no coloured individuals at all. We should have a situation much like that described above. All the colour words would be non-significant, which is to say, there would be no colours. *A fortiori*, if there were no individuals at all, there would be no colours, and more generally, no properties at all. Thus the significance of primitive predicates and (what is the same thing) the existence of the corresponding properties depends upon the existence of individuals. If there were no individuals there would be no descriptive properties, either up in the Platonic heaven or anywhere else. (I should perhaps make it clear that I am maintaining that the existence of Red, for example, is *ante rem* in that it does *not* depend on the existence of red individuals, but is *in re* in that it *does* depend on the existence of coloured individuals.)

Now to return to description-languages, in which '$\sim(\exists x)(x = x)$' is synthetic and appears to express a possible (but non-actual) state of affairs. *If it were true* then all the descriptive predicates of the language would be deprived of significance and would drop out. Thus the language would reduce to a pure calculus and would be deprived of the resources for making it clear that '$\sim(\exists x)(x = x)$' is not "about" an abstract domain of the sort considered by students of purely formal systems, but is "about" a concrete world, which, supposing the formula to be true, does not happen to be there for anything to be "about". In short, in a descriptive language, '$\sim(\exists x)(x = x)$' is rather like 'Everything is red' in that its truth would undermine its significance. On this account we may say that '$\sim(\exists x)(x = x)$' does not genuinely express the possibility of there being no individuals and that '$(\exists x)$ $(x = x)$' does not genuinely record the fact that there are. In view of the fact that descriptive languages are unsatisfactory from a broader point of view[7] we may drop the word 'genuinely' and take it that if there were no individuals, there would be *no* languages in which it would be possible to say so, and that there is no language which succeeds in recording in a synthetic sentence the fact that there are individuals.

Actually, a moment's thought will convince us that if there were no individuals (i.e., if there were no concrete world) there would simply be no languages at all. For a descriptive language (as distinct from either a pure or descriptive calculus) is, by definition, an interpreted language and if there were no concrete world there would be no possibility of supplying an interpretation. Hence no languages. This argument appeals to no particular conception of the nature of languages, but the fact that the result follows immediately from the account of languages given in chapter v lends some support to that account. Obviously, if there were no individuals, properties, and propositions, there would be no class of couples qualifying as a DP, there would be no structures and *a fortiori*, no languages.

We have it, then, that the sentence, 'No individuals exist' (or its symbolic translation, '$\sim(\exists x)(x = x)$') does not describe a possible state of affairs, nor does the sentence, 'There are individuals' ('$(\exists x)(x = x)$') record a fact. This result is a little embarrassing. I have frequently used the locution, 'If there were no individuals then . . .'. If the ante-

[7]My complaints have been registered in *Proper Names*.

cedent is self-contradictory (which, strictly speaking, it is) then the whole conditional is trivially true on any reasonable interpretation of the subjunctive conditional. If I was trying to refer to a possible state of affairs then I was writing nonsense. It is to be hoped that it falls under the heading of useful nonsense because I intend to write a good deal more of it before I am finished.

I shall immediately write more nonsense in order to look at the situation more broadly. We have at least one fact that cannot be recorded synthetically in language: the fact that there are individuals. If there should turn out to be several such facts it might be worth while to coin the term 'proto-fact' to refer to them. Languages are characterized by a descriptive incompleteness comparable to the logical incompleteness established by Gödel's Theorem. According to that theorem, there is an area of logical truth which eludes proof in the system. Here we have an area of fact which eludes description in synthetic sentences of the system. However, the two incompletenesses are inverse rather than parallel. We can *see* that the sentence *17 gen r* must necessarily be true even though we are at a loss to prove it. Here we can prove '$(\exists x)(x = x)$' and according to received doctrines the sentence therefore says nothing. And yet we *see* that it does say something and that we ought not to be able to prove it. In both cases the paradoxes have something to do with self-reference. In the case of the Gödel result a sentence is able to say that what it says is not provably so. Here we have the impossibility of a language talking about itself in anything but sentences which are analytic or self-contradictory. The language cannot synthetically record the existence of individuals because the existence of individuals is a condition of its own existence. The reason why the language can prove that there are individuals is that *given* the existence of itself (a contingent fact) then there *have* to be individuals. As Wittgenstein might have put it, existence can be shown but not said. So far as I know, this is the only view which manages to avoid taking existence as a funny kind of essence.

And since it is a contingent fact that descriptive expressions have significance, we might expect it to be a contingent fact that they signify what they do signify. Since I do not mean simply that it is a contingent fact that Anglo-Saxons use 'Chicago' to signify Chicago, the foregoing statement is oracular, but I shall have to leave it at that for the moment.

We may now look for further proto-facts. Ramsey's quotation from Wittgenstein to the effect that the number of individuals can only be shown suggests that the number of individuals is a proto-fact.

And it is. At any rate the fact that there are at least so many individuals is a proto-fact.

Suppose we have a language with just four individual constants, '*a*', '*b*', '*c*' and '*d*'. And suppose '*a* ≠ *b*', '*a* ≠ *c*', '*a* ≠ *d*', '*b* ≠ *c*', '*b* ≠ *d*', '*c* ≠ *d*' are analytic in the language. They will be descriptively analytic, be it noted. Now we can derive:

$$(\exists x)(\exists y)(\exists z)(\exists u)(x \neq y \,\&\, x \neq z \,\&\, x \neq u \,\&\, y \neq z \,\&\, y \neq u \,\&\, z \neq u)$$

which means that there are at least four distinct individuals. This statement is not logically true (not by D20 and D39 of chapter v, at any rate) but nevertheless is descriptively analytic and, as such, is necessarily true. It is derivable from the nature of the language, in the sense that it is part of the nature of the language that its four individual constants signify (or G-designate) distinct individuals. Yet we think of it as a contingent fact that there are at least four individuals. Thus in analogy to:

If as a matter of fact there are individuals, then necessarily ($\supset \Box$) there are individuals

we have

If as a matter of fact there are at least four individuals, then necessarily ($\supset \Box$) there are at least four individuals.

The same considerations which lead us to regard the existence of individuals as a proto-fact would lead us to regard the existence of at least four individuals as a proto-fact.

Moreover, although we may consider Wittgenstein and Ramsey wrong in trying to define quantification, we can see *why* they were led to make the attempt. Suppose that the G-designata of '*a*', '*b*', '*c*' and '*d*' are all the individuals there are. We might attempt to define '$(x)(Fx)$' and '$(\exists x)(Fx)$' respectively as

(3) $(x)(Fx) =_{df} Fa \,\&\, Fb \,\&\, Fc \,\&\, Fd.$

(4) $(\exists x)(Fx) =_{df} Fa \lor Fb \lor Fc \lor Fd.$

The objection—and it is decisive—is this: We want the left-hand side of (3) to mean that all individuals are *F*, and even supposing that *a*, *b*, *c*, and *d* are all the individuals there are, there is nothing on the RHS of the definition to *say* that these are all the individuals there are. Thus the offered definitions will not do.

But let us consider the statement:

(5) $(x)(Px) \equiv Pa \ \& \ Pb \ \& \ Pc \ \& \ Pd.$

And let us consider a semi-infinite mind, a mind acquainted with all proto-facts but totally ignorant of all recordable contingent facts. That is, if it is a question of knowing what individuals exist, what properties and relations exist and what propositions exist, our semi-infinite mind is omniscient, but if it is a question of knowing which synthetic propositions are true and which false, then he is in darkest ignorance. Yet supposing that *a*, *b*, *c*, and *d* are all the individuals there are, then our semi-infinite mind, notwithstanding its ignorance of contingent fact, could see that (5) *has* to be true. Thus, subject to the supposition mentioned, (5) would be necessarily true. Perhaps this is why Wittgenstein regarded universally quantified propositions as infinite conjunctions of instances. If the foregoing discussion fails to make complete contact with Wittgenstein it is because whereas he thinks in terms of propositional logic, we are here working in terms of sentential or symbolic logic. Nevertheless, perhaps enough has been said to enable us to conclude that the attempt to define quantifiers by connectives represented a genuine insight.

While I myself have no particular wish to wave a banner, it could plausibly be maintained that with the area of proto-facts we have a vindication of metaphysics. Ordinary facts endow sentences with truth or falsity. Proto-facts endow them with significance. Ordinary facts constitute the subject matter of common observation and the special sciences. Proto-facts may be regarded as the subject matter of metaphysics. Furthermore, the notion of a proto-fact might be useful when it comes to dealing with systems or frameworks as a whole and the acceptance or rejection of them. If we want to reject 'This sense-datum is green' we may not want to accept 'This sense-datum is not green'. (*Cf.* Wilfrid Sellars, *Empiricism.*) We may want to reject the whole framework, that is, the proto-facts presupposed by the framework. Disagreement over the choice of a framework is substantive, it is not just a matter of subjective preference.

§26. THE PROTO-FACT THAT THE WORLD IS FOUR-DIMENSIONAL

We shall want to find further proto-facts and the best place to find them is in the woods of conventionalism. I might mention that as regards ordinary logical necessity I am myself a pretty thorough-going conventionalist. And I think it must be said that conventionalism has rendered an important service in impressing us with the very real freedom we enjoy in affirming or denying certain things. Yet there are limits to that freedom and we must do our best to locate those limits as exactly as possible.

In his paper, *Ontology* (p. 29), Carnap discusses the considerations which guide us in the construction of a language.

> Our choice of certain features, although itself not theoretical, is suggested by theoretical knowledge, either logical or factual. For example, the choice of real numbers rather than rational numbers or integers as coordinates is not much influenced by the facts of experience but mainly due to considerations of mathematical simplicity. . . . On the other hand, the decision to use three rather than two or four spatial coordinates is strongly suggested, but still not forced upon us, by the result of common observations. If certain events allegedly observed in spiritualistic seances, e.g., a ball moving out of a sealed box, were confirmed beyond any reasonable doubt, it might seem advisable to use four spatial coordinates.

Carnap obviously regards it as a matter of convention, not as a matter of fact, that our space-time universe is four-dimensional. The scientist simply finds it convenient to use a language whose individual expressions are quadruples of real number expressions. (See also Carnap's *Syntax* p. 307, statements 50a and 50b.) It is claimed that we are not forced to this procedure; we might make do with a language of triples or allow ourselves the luxury of a language of quintuples. I shall deal with the contention about triples and the contention about quintuples in turn.

(*a*) If his thesis is to be saved from triviality, Carnap must mean that given a language whose individual expressions are quadruples of real number expressions (what I shall call a four–co-ordinate language), we could drop the fourth term of these quadruples (thus changing to triples) *without compensating adjustment* and yet not impair the effectiveness of the language. By a 'compensating adjustment' I mean something like this: In the original language a singular fact would be recorded in a sentence of the form, 'the position (x, y, z, t) is P'. If we were to use triples the same fact would be recorded by a sentence of the form 'the place (x, y, z) is P at time t'. The introduction of the time expression on the predicate side of the copula is what I would call a compensating adjustment. Doubtless we could manage with pairs rather than triples provided we made still further compensating adjustments (i.e., something like, '54°N, 120°W is cloudy at 6500 ft. at 1.30 A.M.'). But it would seem clear that we cannot, without compensation, tamper with the degree of the n-tuples to be used as individual expressions without making the language unworkable. Given that only quality words may appear on the predicate side of the copula, then the choice of *n*-tuples of at least fourth degree is genuinely forced upon us. This is what would be meant by those of us who regard it as a matter of brute fact that the world is at least four-dimensional. But of course the stipulation that only quality words may appear on the predicate side of the copula is itself purely conventional. I shall say that a language constructed in accordance with this convention is a *pure* co-ordinate language (in contradistinction to a language "with adjustments"). It is to keep the discussion manageable that I shall adopt this convention and consider only pure co-ordinate languages. To put the matter briefly, I am arguing that a pure co-ordinate language *must* be a four–co-ordinate language.

A pure three–co-ordinate language might be interpreted in such a way that it could record the state of the world at some arbitrarily chosen moment. But it would have nothing to say about the world at different moments. Let us for the moment forget about the account of languages offered in chapter v and let us use the term 'structurally inadequate' to characterize a "language" of the kind just described. The qualifying word 'structurally' is intended to distinguish the inadequacy in question from the sort discussed by Alice Ambrose in *Inadequacy*. For example, a language containing only six colour words, 'red', 'orange', and so on, could not record the fact that this pimpernel is scarlet and not crimson. This kind of inadequacy—incapacity to reflect what C. I. Lewis calls the infinite specificity of the world—is probably to be found in all languages. But the point is this: In regard to the fact that this pimpernel is scarlet, the language mentioned can at least say something, namely, that it is red; whereas in the case of a structurally inadequate language there are facts which it cannot describe in even general terms.

(*b*) Let us hold the notion of structural inadequacy in reserve for a moment and consider the possibility of using a five–co-ordinate language, the first four terms of its standard individual expressions being spatial and the fifth temporal. What are we to make of the fourth spatial co-ordinate? Carnap suggests that if balls moved out of sealed boxes it would be possible to interpret it. (I am not clear as to how the interpretation would be carried out.) But if as a matter of *fact* there occur no phenomena comparable to balls moving out of sealed boxes, then it will simply not be possible to provide a non-trivial interpretation of the fourth spatial co-ordinate. This is what would be meant by those of us who regard it as a matter of fact that the world is at most four-dimensional. By a trivial interpretation I should mean something like this: It might be specified that a sentence of the form, '(x,y,z,u,t) is P' shall mean the same as '(x,y,z,t) is P'. This interpretation is trivial in the sense of being non-differential: it makes no difference to the meaning (i.e., truth conditions) of the sentence what number expression appears in the fourth place of the individual expression. Given sufficient ingenuity it might be possible to provide a differential interpretation of the fourth spatial co-ordinate but it seems clear that no amount of ingenuity will succeed in interpreting it in a manner homogeneous with either the other three spatial co-ordinates or the temporal co-ordinate. There being no *differential, homogeneous* interpretation possible for the fourth co-ordinate, I shall call a five–co-ordinate language 'structurally redundant'.

I have been concerned to argue that if we wish a *structurally adequate and non-redundant pure co-ordinate* language, then the choice of a four–co-ordinate language is forced on us by the brute fact that the world is four-dimensional. But how are we synthetically to record this fact, brutal or otherwise? Three possibilities suggest themselves. Since none of them work, we shall find ourselves swinging back in Carnap's direction.

1. I am not sure how one would say in a pure four–co-ordinate language that space-time is four-dimensional, but the following might be a reasonable attempt:

$$(x)(\exists n_i)(\exists n_j)(\exists n_k)(\exists n_l)[x = (n_i, n_j, n_k, n_l)].$$

Unfortunately it is analytic in the language in question. Attempts to say that space-time is three-dimensional or five-dimensional would be self-contradictory (or perhaps non-significant). The discussion here is bound to be somewhat imprecise and inconclusive, because there are some questions raised by the fact that the individual expressions of a four–co-ordinate language are not unitary expressions, but quadruples of real number expressions. What do the single real number expressions refer to, real numbers or distances from axes? These questions leave me with a feeling that the whole notion of a co-ordinate language is a little problematical, but not so problematical as to prevent us from making some use of it.

2. We might leave aside co-ordinate languages and, concentrating on the three-dimensionality of space, say, "It is impossible to place four rods mutually at right angles." The difficulty here is in making sense out of the word 'impossible'. What we have is not a kind of physical impossibility like the impossibility of making silk purses

out of sows' ears or that of constructing a perpetual motion machine. There are physical laws which entail 'It is not the case that there is a perpetual-motion machine' but there are no physical laws entailing 'There do not exist four rods mutually at right angles'. Rather, it is the impossibility of giving a specific description of what it would be like to have four rods mutually at right angles. Let us suppose we have imposed a three–co-ordinate system on physical space, then we can say, "Let one end of rod A be at place——, let the other be at ——. Let one end of rod B be at ——, the other at ——. Let one end of rod C be at ——, the other at ——." Assuming that the blanks have been filled in with co-ordinates such as to make A, B, and C mutually at right angles, it would be easy to prove that whatever co-ordinates are chosen for the ends of rod D, D is not at right angles to all the other three rods. Again, then, the attempt to express the four-dimensionality of space-time (here the three-dimensionality of space) yields a sentence which is analytic. And attempts to express the possibility of the world being five-dimensional yield results which are self-contradictory (or perhaps non-significant).

The reason I keep repeating, "self-contradictory (or perhaps non-significant)" is this: If the language has triples of real number expressions referring to places in (three-) space then it is provably false that there are eight places such that if four rods have their ends at these places they are mutually at right angles. But the "language" might use quadruples instead of triples, in which case one could go through the motions of giving a description of four rods mutually at right angles and, moreover, "prove" (given the "places" of the ends of the rods) that they are at right angles. But the point is that the fourth spatial co-ordinates have no significance; there is no co-ordinating definition for them. We can make some kind of sense out of 'north of', 'east of', and 'above', but we could not make any sense out of any other directional word which was supposed to be independent of but somehow co-ordinate with these three expressions. Thus the alleged description of four rods mutually at right angles is non-significant. It does not describe a real possibility.

3. And so let us make the trek to the metalanguage. The statement, 'L_1 is a four–co-ordinate language' will not do as a synthetic record of the fact that the world is four-dimensional, because it would be provable on the definition of 'L_1'. What we want to say is that any structurally adequate and non-redundant pure co-ordinate language must be a four–co-ordinate language. But any suitable definition of 'structurally adequate and non-redundant' would have to entail that

a structurally adequate and non-redundant pure co-ordinate language must use n-tuples of the same degree as there are dimensions in the world. Now the metalanguage actually *used* in chapter v was a pure language. But what was *envisaged* was a language fleshed out with descriptive expressions so as to make possible the definition of specific languages. And if the non-semantical parts of M are structurally adequate and non-redundant it would be possible to prove *a priori* that any structurally adequate and non-redundant pure co-ordinate language is a four–co-ordinate language. We still have no synthetic record of the fact we are trying to record. (I suppose that in the pure metalanguage used in chapter v the result in question would not be provable and we could maintain that such a language *can* record the fact that the world is four-dimensional. But it cannot record any ordinary contingent facts.)

As a last desperate effort we might leave 'structurally adequate and non-redundant' undefined at this level and frame a definition of 'scientist X finds L structurally adequate and non-redundant' at the psychological level. Our definiens might be something like 'X is happy in the use of L'. The impossible paradox here is that whereas we begin by trying to talk about the dimensional order of space-time, we should end up talking about the psychological attitudes of scientists towards various types of language.

We may conclude, along with Carnap, that statements about the four-dimensionality of the world are analytic. I hesitate to add "but contingently meaningful" because the situation here is obviously more complicated than in the case of '$(\exists x)(x = x)$'. Contingency comes in with the *fact* that a given *whole language* in regard to its atomic formation rules is or is not structurally adequate and non-redundant. We may put the matter this way: if as a matter of fact the world has precisely four dimensions, then necessarily ('$\supset \square$' not '$\rightarrow$') the world has precisely four dimensions. The earlier gloss on Ramsey (p. 101) was made with one eye on the present discussion. The four-dimensionality of space-time is a proto-fact. It can be shown by the structure of the language but not said in the language.

We may now pick up certain questions left up in the air in chapter v. Let us suppose that in seeking a definition of 'language' we shall want a definition which will ensure that all structures covered by the definition shall be structurally adequate and non-redundant. So far as I can see, this requirement is not entailed by C2 and C3, but it would seem to be reasonable in any case. The requirement has actually been satisfied through D6, which states that an expression is an atomic sentence if and only if it G-designates a G-proposition. Now

G-propositions are correlated with atomic facts in the sense that an atomic fact is a true G-proposition. And the degree of complexity of an atomic fact (it is a proto-fact that an atomic fact has *that* degree of complexity) will come to be reflected in the complexity of an atomic sentence through R5, the regularity requirement.

The reason why we defined 'atomic sentence' in terms of G-propositions, rather than conversely, is precisely because we wished the influence to flow from G-propositions to sentences and not in the reverse direction. It is as if, lacking very many preconceptions about formation rules, we recognized that atomic facts have a certain nature or degree of complexity in their own right and that atomic sentences must mirror that complexity. It should be noted that chapter v is entirely noncommittal as to the nature of atomic fact.

The reason why intensional propositions will not serve in general semantics is not so much that they contain individual concepts rather than ordinary individuals, but rather that *intension* is a purely syntactical concept. Whether we do or do not recognize intensions as entities, *having the same intension* would be defined through the syntactical concept of logical equivalence. And so long as all that matters is that there shall be rules governing the logical equivalence of sentences, there is nothing to prevent us laying down formation rules *ad libitum*. We might have formation rules according to which, with 'Philip II' and 'drunk' provided with the expected designation rules, the expression 'Philip is drunk' qualifies as a sentence. (The copula 'is' is always tenseless.[8]) The objection would be as follows: In saying 'Philip is drunk' you are not saying anything which can be true or false. You have to say something like 'Philip is drunk at three in the afternoon of April 1, 350 B.C.', or—existential generalization on the foregoing—'Philip is drunk at some time' (which, according to legend, is true). Philip II is a three-dimensional entity.[9] Since the world is four-dimensional the sentence in question must have in addition an expression referring to the fourth dimension, so that it may have a degree of complexity corresponding with that of fact and thereby say something which can be true or false.[10] The *simpliste* character of the foregoing argument should not conceal its cogency and its importance.

[8]Tensed verbs are egocentric. The problem of egocentricity belongs to pragmatics and we shall keep clear of it here. My remarks on semantics, pragmatics, and egocentricity in *Identity* are more than a little confused.

[9]This would be made clear by axioms of individuation such as are given in my *Space*.

[10]Precisely the same observations could be made on 'Chicago is large'. Thus L_2 of chapter iii is not really a language at all. In Chapter iii, I permitted myself some semantic oversimplification in order to concentrate on logical questions.

It shows, quite decisively I think, that we must somehow break away from formation rules conceived on purely conventionalistic-syntactical lines.[11]

It may have been noticed that in chapter V, once we had defined 'designative', most of the remaining definitions and requirements were purely syntactical in character, making no reference to designation. The exceptions were D6, which defined 'atomic sentence', and the regularity requirement, R5. It is by D6 that we break out of the narrow circle of syntax and make contact with reality. And it is G-propositions that enable us to make the break. G-propositions put us to the trouble of recognizing simple defined properties, of having property descriptions of the second sort and of complicating our formation and transformation rules with elaborate stipulations regarding the placing of description scope symbols. But in the long run they are worth the trouble.

§27. SENSE AND SENSIBILITY[12]

If the reader finds himself profoundly dissatisfied with the trend of §§25 and 26, he has all my sympathy. This is the kind of question which naturally comes to mind: If it is logically true that there are individuals, then the statement that there are no individuals is logically false. Does that mean (it will be asked) that I cannot conceive of the non-existence of the world? Then what becomes of Schopenhauer and his contention that "The uneasiness which keeps the never-resting clock of metaphysics in motion, is the consciousness that the non-existence of the world is just as possible as its existence"?[13] Again, it is claimed that it is analytically true that the world is four-dimensional. Does this mean that we cannot conceive of a world of three or five dimensions? But surely an ingenious science fiction writer might spin a tale about people living in a five-dimensional world.

[11]The *simpliste* argument is not new. "Some judgments . . . contain an explicit or implicit reference to time. But this is really part of the judgment. As soon as the judgment is fully stated it becomes independent of time. It may perhaps be said that the judgment *France is under Bourbon rule* was true two centuries ago, but is not true now. But the judgment as it stands, without context, is incompletely stated. That France is (or was) under Bourbon rule in the year 1906 A.D. is for all time false; that France is (or was) under Bourbon rule in the year 1706 A.D. is for all time true." J. N. Keynes, *Studies and Exercises in Formal Logic*, 4th ed., 1906, pp. 76–7. Quoted in A. N. Prior, *Time and Modality*, Oxford, 1957, p. 108.

[12]*Pace* Miss Jane Austen.

[13]Quoted by William James in his paper, "The Sentiment of Rationality," *Essays in Pragmatism*, ed. Alburey Castel, Hafner, 1951, p. 9.

And sooner or later we shall have to put Cerberus on a leash. It may have been noticed that in chapter v it was laid down that all individual constants are designative (i.e., G-designate entities). Languages as herein defined do not contain non-naming names like 'Pegasus' and 'Cerberus', and we have one more shortcoming to chalk up against D39. My neglect of Pegasus and Cerberus was motivated by systematic considerations. It was not due to any lack of admiration for these estimable beasts or to an insensitiveness to the problem raised by putative proper names. On the contrary, the problem seems to me to be more general.

Let us invent a new concept, which we may call 'sense'. Whatever I say in what follows, and however I say it, I do not intend to suggest that there is an entity which is the sense of an expression. Briefly, the sense of a name (whether individual constant or predicate constant) is a function of what is said about the alleged nominatum (or designatum). For instance, if I were to say, "Cerberus is a man with a long white beard who lives at the north pole. Cerberus wears a red coat. Cerberus runs a non-union toy factory. Every year on the evening of December 24, he flies about on a reindeer-drawn sleigh, climbs down chimneys and leaves toys for children," you might reply, "Oh, you don't mean Cerberus, you mean Santa Claus." Since I assert the same things about Cerberus as you assert about Santa Claus, the name 'Cerberus' has the same *sense* for me as 'Santa Claus' has for you.[14] But neither word has significance. We may say, however, that the words 'Cerberus' and 'Santa Claus' are *sensible* (i.e., senseful).

Of course even *significant* (i.e., designative) names get their sense in the same way. I may make a number of synthetic assertions about Socrates and these assertions determine the sense which the name 'Socrates' has for me. A class of assertions can be abstracted from the person or group which makes the assertions. What I meant earlier (p. 105) in saying that it is a contingent fact that significant names signify what they do signify is this: given the sense of a name, that is, given a set of synthetic assertions containing the name, then it would require an empirical investigation to discover whether it signifies anything and what it signifies.

Presumably if one says enough about God, then the word 'God' is thereby endowed with at least sense.

Predicates have sense in much the same way, that is, by things

[14]Of course you do not believe what you say about Santa Claus, nor I what I have said about Cerberus. And so 'assertion' has to be taken in the weak sense of 'things said about, with or without credence'.

being asserted using the predicates. Not being a professional chemist I have no definition of the predicate 'gold'. Yet I may make a number of assertions about gold.

(6)	Gold is a metal.
(7)	Gold is yellowish.
(8)	Gold does not tarnish.
(9)	Gold is precious and is used in making jewelry.
(10)	The Incas had more gold than iron.
(11)	Gold dissolves in *aqua regia*.
(12)	Gold is an element with atomic number 79.
(13)	Gold has a specific gravity of 19.2.

Statement (6) is probably analytic, but all the others are synthetic (for me, that is). I can quite easily conceive of any of (7)–(13) being false. These statements define the *sense* which the word 'gold' has for me. It is of course a contingent fact that 'gold' signifies a property. (And I don't mean that it is a contingent fact that *I* use the word 'gold' to signify a property; I mean that it is a contingent fact that 'gold', determined as to its sense by (6)–(13), signifies a property.) The element of contingency here is brought out by the possibility of constructing predicates which, like 'Pegasus' and 'Cerberus', have sense but no significance.

Consider the predicate '*P*', which a person might use in a number of synthetic assertions.

(14)	*P* is a metal.
(15)	*P* turns base metals into gold.
(16)	*P* is jet black.
(17)	*P* is mined exclusively in the Sahara Desert.
(18)	*P* has a specific gravity of 15.7.
(19)	Cerberus has a dog collar made out of *P*.

These assertions endow the expression '*P*' with sense, but an empirical investigation would disclose that there is no such property as *P* and that '*P*', like 'Pegasus' and 'Cerberus', is non-significant.[15]

The possibility of having putative property names seems to me to render abortive the attempt to assimilate bogus individual names like 'Cerberus' to genuine names like 'Socrates' and to construe all names as abbreviations for definite descriptions.[16] The manœuvre

---

[15]The foregoing is intended to make good the 'I shall state without present argument' gambit used toward the bottom of p. 76 of *Proper Names*.

[16]See Quine, *ML*, 1st ed., pp. 149 ff., *Methods*, pp. 215 ff.

fails to take account of precisely the same difficulty as it arises in connection with bogus property names. If we followed the same procedure with predicates, treating them as abbreviations of definite descriptions (e.g., Blue $=_{df}$ the colour of the sky) then we should have our individual expressions and predicates taking in each other's wash. The nominalist, of course, does not have to worry about the considerations just adduced because he holds that *no* predicate names an entity. But so far as I can see it is not possible to obtain a general definition of 'language' within the framework of nominalism, and such a definition seems to me to be more desirable than the kind of economy nominalism aims at.

So much, then, by way of a rough outline of sense and sensibility. Logical signs, of course, have no sense. Their significance is their intension (I do not mean that there is an entity which is the intension of a logical sign!) and significance is the only dimension of meaning that a logical sign has. We may now add a few remarks on the relationship between sense and significance. (And by 'significance' I always mean 'as explicated for primitive descriptive signs by G-designation'.)

If the enterprise of general semantics is defined by convention C2 (p. 19) then we cannot use sense as a basic notion. That is, we cannot take it that two languages are identical only if the descriptive expressions have the same sense in both languages. The objection is the same as the objection to using *intension*. Sir Thomas More and Horace Walpole assert vastly different things about Richard III. Therefore a different sense attaches to the name in their respective languages. If we supposed that the languages are therefore different and (by C2) that these two people would fail to intercommunicate, then we are, in effect, supposing that More and Walpole could not argue about the question as to whether Richard III really was responsible for the murder of the princes in the Tower. But that is absurd.

And we find in any case that there are at least two respects in which significance takes priority over sense. The first has to do with truth conditions. Let us go back and pick up the attempt to describe a five-dimensional world. We have already said that such a description would be non-significant. We may say, however, that it is *sensible*. But if we ask, "Is such a description true or false?" we find ourselves puzzled. To say that it is false would suggest—erroneously—that the world is five-dimensional but does not happen to have the character attributed to it in the description. We may conclude that, notwithstanding the fact that a description of a five-dimensional world may have sense, it nevertheless (as a matter of fact or proto-fact) *has no truth and falsity conditions.* This shows that significance is much closer than sensibility to the traditional notion of meaningfulness. And suppose we ask, "Is the sentence, 'Pegasus eats oats' true or false?" The answer, "It is true", is obviously wrong and at the same time the answer, "It is false", is misleading in that it suggests that Pegasus eats something else. There are of course alternatives, but it seems to me preferable to say that this sentence has no truth conditions and therefore no truth value. And *within* G, we should appeal to the proto-fact that there is no such G-proposition as the G-proposition that Pegasus eats oats (there being no such individual as Pegasus).

The second respect in which significance takes priority over sense has to do with the dependence of the latter on the former. I mentioned a moment ago that if one says enough about God, then the word 'God' is thereby endowed with at least sense, the inference being that if one says enough about anything, the word in question is given sense. This is not entirely correct. For in making statements about Pegasus and Cerberus we do in fact apply significant predicates to them, and in making statements about the fictional property P, we used expressions which were either significant or else had sense independently. And our science fiction writer, composing his non-significant story about a five-dimensional world, presumably has to use *some* significant expressions. Thus if any expressions are to have sense, some expressions must have significance and significance is the primary concept. That is why it is reasonable to attempt to explicate significance (through *language* and *G-designation*) even if it means temporarily neglecting sensible, non-significant expressions like 'Pegasus' and 'Cerberus'. The dependence of the sensibility of some expressions on the significance of others can be made clear by the following example:

> 'Twas brillig, and the slithy toves
> Did gyre and gimble in the wabe:
> All mimsy were the borogoves,
> And the mome raths outgrabe.

The passage appears to say quite a lot about quite a number of things. Nevertheless it is *utterly* senseless (in English) for the very simple reason that none of the descriptive expressions have significance (in English).

But having said that no expression has sense unless some expressions have significance I shall want to qualify even *that*. I conjecture that it would be possible to frame a world description having sense quite apart from the significance of any non-logical expressions.

The non-logical expressions would derive their sense from the syntactical relations obtaining among them. The question, "What conditions must a world description satisfy if it is to have sense, even though lacking significance?" seems to me to be a *really* interesting question. For if we had an answer we should have a genuine insight into the nature of individuals, qualities, and relations, in the sense of having a full intellectualization of the world of sense perception. As things stand now, about the best that can be done with the question, "What *is* Red?" is to say, "Red is an ineffable quality. All you can do is point to examples of it." This can scarcely pass as the last word philosophy has to say on the subject.

The reason I made the conjecture regarding the possibility of sensible, non-significant world descriptions is this: I should conjecture that the *real* features of the world are its structural features, that is, the world *is* pure structure. And I make this conjecture because, if the world contained a pure quality, having no internal relations to any other qualities, then it would make no practical difference if that quality were replaced in all its instances by a different pure quality. Or if the world contained a set of qualities having internal relations among each other, then it would make no practical difference if that set were replaced in all their instances by a different set provided the relations were kept invariant. *If* the world is pure structure, then it ought to be possible to describe it using expressions whose meanings can be characterized in a *purely formal way*. This, of course, is syntactics with such a vengeance as to bring us back almost to Absolute Idealism and some form of an ontological argument for the existence of the world. All that would be necessary would be to suppose, in addition, that for reasons determinable *a priori*, just one world description could be sensible independently of the significance of any of its expressions.

The concept of sense really belongs in what I should call "secondary semantics" and a full discussion of it would require another book.[17] Yet it seemed desirable to give some indication in this work of a method of handling non-naming names in G. If we are deeply concerned about Pegasus and Cerberus we can add a fifth term to languages as we now understand them. (The first four terms are, in order, the descriptive part, the logical part, the definitional superstructure, and the mathematical superstructure.) The fifth term, which

---

[17]In secondary semantics more extensive use is made of 'co-designative' rather than 'G-designates' and the descriptive portions of *M* wither away. A rough indication of what is conceived to be the peculiar technique of secondary semantics is given in my *Rules*, pp. 95–6, especially the second full paragraph on p. 96.

might be called "the fictional superstructure", would be a class of classes of sentences. A set of sentences containing 'Pegasus' might be one such class, a set of sentences containing 'Cerberus' might be another such set. It would have to be understood that these non-naming names are not replaceable by quantifiable variables. Moreover there would be no truth conditions for sentences of the fictional superstructure. We should have it that two languages are identical only if they have the same non-naming names and these non-naming names have the same sense in both languages, that is, the same class of synthetic assertions. This is perhaps an excessively stringent criterion, but I doubt that it would be worth the trouble to attempt to relax it.

VII. A PROGRAMME FOR PRAGMATICS

§28. LANGUAGE DESCRIPTIONS

Chapter VI dealt with relatively advanced matters. I now wish to return to the elementary account of language given in chapter V. There is a question as to the possibility of framing a definition of 'language' which would cover, say, English, French, and German. We might arrive at such a definition by relaxing some of the requirements listed in chapter V. Or we might define a different sense of 'language' by taking a language to be a mapping of expressions onto sentences of some language as defined by D39. We should, of course, have to impose a regularity requirement and this would prove a matter of some difficulty. I shall not follow up either of these suggestions. Instead, I shall blandly assume that English, French, and German are entities like—or at least "sufficiently" like—the entities defined by D39. It will be argued subsequently that it matters scarcely at all that this assumption happens to be false. It is worth remarking here that I propose to replace the distinction between natural and artificial languages—a distinction which has never been drawn, incidentally—by a different distinction which will accomplish the same purpose.

Once we conceive of languages as entities of a certain sort—and quantification over language variables would appear to commit us to that conception—then the next obvious step is to distinguish between direct reference to a language by name, and indirect reference to a language by description, just as we elaborated that distinction in the case of properties and propositions. Strictly speaking, languages are "composed" of classes (which are pseudo-entities) and, by the ontological criterion of chapter IV, languages themselves are therefore pseudo-entities and language variables pseudo-range. However, this circumstance in no way militates against framing expressions which are *syntactically* language descriptions, and it will be convenient to continue speaking of languages as entities.

The most common language descriptions are those which describe a language in terms of a person or community who use it, for example, 'the language used by Charles' or 'the language used by Anglo-Saxons' (i.e., 'English'). If Charles in fact uses L_1 (an entirely accidental property of L_1) then the statement,

(1)   the language used by Charles = L_1,

will be a factual statement comparable (apart from type differences) to 'the author of *Waverley* = Walter Scott'. The last part of Church's *Abstract Entities* may be read in this way: Church is defining a little language (let us call it L_4) and is making a factual statement that

(2) L_4 is a sub-language of the language used by Anglo-Saxons.

That the putative language names of ordinary language are really abbreviated language descriptions can be shown from the following considerations. Understanding a language name involves (to put it loosely) knowing the composition of the language. (The foregoing is a loose statement because knowing what a language is could not reasonably be taken to mean being able to identify any given expression-member of its logical part.) But I *understand* the word 'Japanese' as occurring in the statement, 'He speaks Japanese fluently', and yet I do not know what that language is. Being ignorant of Japanese I cannot imagine what it would be like to go to Japan and discover to my astonishment that the Japanese don't speak Japanese. If they speak at all the Japanese *have* (' ㋐ ' not ' ㋡ ㋲') to speak Japanese. The word 'Japanese' must be an abbreviation of 'the language used by the Japanese'. The reason why we are sometimes misled into taking 'English' as a language name is that we are all familiar with its descriptum (as most of us are not familiar with the descriptum of 'Japanese') and when we use the word 'English' we tend to think of the semantical properties of the descriptum rather than the meaning of 'English', just as a person hearing 'the author of *Waverley*' might think of the personal and literary qualities of Walter Scott instead of the meaning of the description. Yet writers are pretty well agreed in regarding, for example,

(3)   'Chicago' designates Chicago in English,

as a factual statement, which is tantamount to conceding that 'English' does not mention any semantical properties but does mention Anglo-Saxons.

And of course we should never in the first place have permitted ourselves to be so careless as to use 'English' and 'French' as nouns allegedly naming "natural" languages. These words are adjectives. What we meant was 'the English language' and 'the French language'. And if 'the French capital' is a description of Paris, it is a little difficult to see what else 'the French language' could be but a description of the language used there.

The foregoing remarks are in a sense the most important in this book. For if the question is raised, "Is the enterprise of the book—all the tedious business of chapter v—worthwhile?" then the answer is to be found here. Whether we are aware of it or not we do use language descriptions, which contain an iota and a variable '*L*'. And we must have a clear answer to the question, "What are the values of the variable '*L*'?"

The distinction between naming and describing a language is immediately helpful in connection with at least two problems. We may utilize this distinction to preserve the essentials of Carnap's analysis of statements of assertion and belief (in *M & N*, §§13, 14) against the apparently overwhelming difficulties adduced by Church (in *Assertion*). In his article Church paraphrases Carnap for purposes of exposition and I shall take the same liberty in paraphrasing the argument into the jargon of this book. Suppose we have the sentence:

(4)   Seneca said that man is a rational animal.

Its translation into German is presumably:

(5)   Seneca hat gesagt dass der Mensch ein vernünftiges Tier ist.

We have the following paraphrase of Carnap's proposed analysis of (4):

(6)   There is a sentence S_1 in a language L such that (*a*) S_1 in L is intensionally isomorphic to 'Man is a rational animal' in English, and (*b*) Seneca wrote S_1 in L.

Similarly, (5) expands into:

(7)   Es gibt einen Satz S_1 in einer Sprache L, so dass (*a*) S_1 auf L intensional isomorph zu 'Der Mensch ist ein vernünftiges Tier' auf Deutsch ist, und (*b*) Seneca S_1 auf L geschrieben hat.

The difficulty is that (7) is not a translation of (6). Statement (6) would presumably translate as:

(8)   Es gibt einen Satz S_1 in einer Sprache L, so dass (*a*) S_1 auf L intensional isomorph zu 'Man is a rational animal' auf Englisch ist, und (*b*) Seneca S_1 auf L geschrieben hat.

Clearly, (8) would not convey to a German ignorant of English what (6) conveys to an Englishman. And the reason is not far to seek. 'English' is a description and the German is not familiar, as the Englishman is, with its descriptum. In the same way, 'The author of

Waverley is Scotch' conveys less to a person who does not know that the author of *Waverley* is Walter Scott than to a person who does have that information.

And so what we must do is replace these language descriptions by language names defined in terms of the composition of the language. If from (6) and (8) we obtain (6') and (8') by replacing 'English' and 'Englisch' by 'L_1' defined as suggested, then when (6') is translated into German the definition of 'L_1' naturally has to be translated into German also. This would be true of any defined technical term in a passage of English given for translation into German. Now if he is given the definition of 'L_1' (8') should convey to a German that Seneca said that all men are rational animals. Further if (7') is obtained from (7) in a similar fashion by replacing 'Deutsch' by 'L_5' (say)—defined by specifying the composition of German, then (7') and (8') are mutual translations in the broad sense of it being possible to determine *a priori* that they have the same truth value. This seems to me to solve the particular problem under discussion. Briefly, statements like (4) and (5) are not admitted into the language, on the ground that (*a*) they give rise to difficulties, and (*b*) statements like (6') and (7') provide us with resources for saying what we might have wanted to say with statements like (4) and (5). I should wish, naturally, to substitute a concept of *significational isomorphism* for the concept of *intensional isomorphism*, but that is a relatively minor point. There are a number of other difficulties to be met in connection with the analysis of statements of belief and the interested reader is referred to Carnap's *Belief* and the articles cited therein. It is of some interest that in order to describe beliefs and assertions we cannot use a lowest order object language but have to move up into a pragmatic metalanguage.

The second problem on which we might well bring our distinction to bear is the problem of analyticity. In the light of the considerations raised earlier we shall do well to abandon the distinction between artificial and natural languages—if there can be such a thing as abandoning an undrawn distinction—and to replace it by a distinction between reference to a language by name (defined in such a way as to give the composition of the language) and reference to it by description. There is presumably a distinction between used and unused languages, but, like the distinction between black horses and white horses, it is of no particular philosophical interest. Descriptive semantics, then, is not the study of natural or historically given languages (Carnap, *Semantics*, pp. 11–12) because the study of any language belongs to pure semantics. Rather it is the study of communicative behaviour with a view to discovering which language it is that is being used in communication.

In any case the use of the phrase 'natural language' has thrown a smoke-screen over the question of the analytic-synthetic distinction and introduced some confusion into the discussions which have followed the publication of White's *Dualism* and Quine's *Dogmas*. The participants tend to write as though there were one problem of analyticity for artificial languages and another for the so-called "natural" languages. It is as if we were to characterize seven, eight, and nine as "artificial" numbers and the number of deadly sins, the number of April Rainers, and the number of planets as "natural" numbers, and then were to talk about one problem of prime factoring "artificial" numbers and wax gloomy over another problem of prime factoring "natural" numbers. Obviously there is a rather complex problem of prime factoring a "natural" number. And in the same way there is perhaps some genuine problem which bothers White and Quine. It remains to be seen if we cannot locate it.

§29. DESCRIPTIVE SEMIOTIC AND THEORETICAL DESCRIPTIVE SEMIOTIC

A moment ago, I rejected Carnap's brief, working account of descriptive semantics, although, strictly speaking, I object less to what Carnap says than to the way in which he says it. In G, descriptive semantics (or preferably, descriptive semiotic) is thought of as a factual science concerned with the truth or falsity of statements like (1):

(1)   the language used by Charles = L_1.

Associated with this statement there will be other statements of two different sorts, for example:

(9)   The couple (E_1, e_1) is a member of the DP (descriptive part) of the language used by Charles.

(10)   The expressions S_1 is an expression-member of the LP (logical part) of the language used by Charles.

By D3 and D20 of chapter v these entail respectively:

(11) E_1 G-designates e_1 in the language used by Charles.

(12) S_1 is logically true in the language used by Charles.

In addition to, and prior to, the science of descriptive semiotic concerned with the truth *values* of the statements given, we shall need an *a priori* science concerned with their meaning or explication, that is, with their truth conditions. That is to say, we shall want general behaviouristic definitions of the following:

FDP1. The language used by person $P = L$.

FDP2. (E,e) is a member of the DP of the language L used by P.

FDP3. S is an expression-member of the LP of the language L used by P.

As before, D3 and D20 permit transitions to:

FDP2'. E G-designates e in the language L used by P.

FDP3'. S is logically true in the language L used by P.

The task of defining FDP3 or FDP3' can be regarded as belonging to an *a priori* science of *theoretical descriptive syntax*. FDP2 or FDP2' belong to *theoretical descriptive semantics*. If we like, we may simply invent a more comprehensive science of *theoretical descriptive semiotic* to take care of all three definienda. And since all three contain reference to the use of a language, this more comprehensive science will be considered as part of pure pragmatics. It is on this account that the definienda are called the *fundamental definienda of pragmatics*.

Once these definitions have been supplied, then presumably we shall have full explications of the semantic concepts (except that of descriptive analyticity). In particular we could claim an explication of languagehood. For the pedagogical requirement (C1, p. 16) would now be satisfied. In teaching Hermann L_1 (= English) one would first make a general statement of what it is for a person to use a language (e.g., something like 'P uses $L =_{df}$ if (E,e) is a member of the DP of L then if P wishes to assert something about e he uses a token of E'). Then one would state the composition of L_1, avoiding the use of the technical jargon of semantics which Hermann does not understand. Now, in principle at least, Hermann should be able to use L_1.

It has already been pointed out that one reason for the barbarous appearance of languages as characterized in chapter v is this: our pre-analytic concepts of *language* and *use of a language* are so inter-confused that *any* attempt to untangle them will yield analyses that separately appear to be counter-intuitive. About the most that we can reasonably demand is that the complete analysis will permit us to say the important things we have been saying at the pre-analytic level. If the programme of theoretical descriptive semiotic were carried out then presumably adequate post-analytic resources would be available for saying what we want to say. And at this point we can at least envisage one possible form of the untangling of pre-analytic concepts. If a final characterization of language were wanted it would run something like this: an entity is a language if it has the general character described in chapter v and in addition has a double disposition: if it were used by a person P then if P were in such and such a situation he would behave in such and such a way.

All this can perhaps be put more clearly by redrawing the map of semiotic. It will be noted that we pass from the more abstract levels of semiotic to the more "concrete" by enriching the metalanguage.

I. Pure Semiotic

A. Pure Syntax: Definitions of 'calculus' and 'logically true'. M contains names of expressions and variables ranging over expressions.

B. Pure (Primary) Semantics: Definitions of 'language', 'G-designates' and 'true'. M contains, in addition, descriptive signs and variables ranging over their designata.

C. Pure Pragmatics (including theoretical descriptive semiotic): Definition of 'uses'. M contains, in addition, variables ranging over language users and resources to describe their behaviour.

II. Descriptive Semiotic

An empirical discipline including both descriptive syntax and descriptive semantics.

It might be mentioned that the field I have been calling 'secondary semantics' is an offshoot of theoretical descriptive semantics.

It is worth noting, too, that FDP2′ can be taken as 'E G-designates (or signifies) e for P'. This last suggests Ogden and Richards and the triangle of reference (*Meaning*, p. 11) and their generally descriptive-psychological approach to semantic problems. The present method can be taken as supplying a bridge between their psychological approach to language *behaviour* and the more formal approach of the academic semanticists. It is a kind of bridge, moreover, which should make it not too difficult to keep clear of both psychologism in logic and logicism in psychology. Psychologism in logic[1] is the view that logic has to do with judgments and inferences, that logic is the art of thinking or the Theory of Inquiry. Actually, logic has no more and no less to do with thinking than mathematics has. The less well-known

[1] See Carnap's excellent discussion, *Probability*, §11.

fallacy of logicism in psychology involves the attribution of causal efficacy to logical properties and relations, as in "Having said that all men are mortal and Socrates is a man, he went on to affirm that Socrates is mortal, *because* the fact that Socrates is mortal *follows from* the fact that all men are mortal and Socrates is a man." The last clause should be written as ". . . because, among other things, he was using a language in which 'Socrates is mortal' is derivable from the sentences 'All men are mortal' and 'Socrates is a man'." If Ryle were willing we might use the term "logicism in psychology" to describe the mistake of applying to thinking processes those logical terms which can be applied sensibly only to the *results* of thinking. (See his *The Concept of Mind*, pp. 285 ff.)

§30. FIRST PERSONAL DESCRIPTIVE SEMIOTIC AND THE PARADOX OF ANALYSIS

I have mentioned that in descriptive semiotic we observe a person's behaviour with a view to finding out what expressions he uses and how he uses them. However, we might introspectively examine our own inclinations regarding the use of words with a view to delineating the character of the language we ourselves use, in which case we are practising what may be called 'first personal descriptive semiotic'. First personal descriptive semiotic lies at the bottom of a good deal of philosophical analysis, and so we are quite close to the paradox of analysis.

Let us suppose that I am concerned to analyse my concept of *brother*, or, if you like, that I am concerned to analyse the significance of the word 'brother' as I use it. I ask myself, "If I were to observe something to which I felt inclined or disposed to apply the term 'brother' would I also feel inclined, on that account alone, to apply the term 'male sibling'? Yes. If I were to observe something to which I felt inclined to apply the term 'male sibling' would I also feel inclined, on that account alone, to apply the term 'brother'? Yes." And so I set up a precisely defined reconstruction of my language in which 'brother ≡ male sibling' is analytic. The equivalence is in some sense informative since I went to some trouble to arrive at it. But—and here is the paradox—if the equivalence is analytically true, then 'brother' and 'male sibling' are synonymous and the equivalence mentioned means the same as the trivial equivalence 'brother ≡ brother'.

Let us call the reconstruction of my language 'L_4'. We have the factual statement,

(13)   The language I habitually use = L_4.

We also have:

(14)   'brother ≡ brother' is analytic in L_4.
(15)   'brother ≡ male sibling' is analytic in L_4.

These are both analytic and as such are equally trivial or equally portentous. But we also have:

(16)   'brother ≡ brother' is analytic in the language I habitually use.
(17)   'brother ≡ male sibling' is analytic in the language I habitually use.

These are both factual statements and therefore *both* informative. It is not difficult to see why the second is more interesting than the first: 'brother' occurs essentially in 'brother ≡ male sibling' but not in 'brother ≡ brother'. The second, I believe, is the statement which analysts find to have an appearance of being informative. It has such an appearance because it *is* informative; this is the statement I take some pains to arrive at.

§31. ACTUAL COMMUNICATIVE BEHAVIOUR

In §§28 and 29 I have assumed, falsely, that all Anglo-Saxons use a single language which accords with the definition of 'language' offered in chapter v. In other words, I have idealized or simplified the actual facts. What I have been doing is considering a semantically ideal community, one which uses a language in the rather narrow sense defined. Their language would be logically precise in the sense that every sentence of it would be either logically true, logically false, or logically indeterminate. Then I suggested that we lay down the descriptive semantic and descriptive syntactic procedures by which we should go about discovering what this language is. This kind of idealization serves the same purpose as frictionless surfaces and perfectly elastic collisions in physics.[2] We can regard the communicative behaviour of the human race as having undergone a process of evolution. Our remote ancestors, swinging from branch to branch, presumably communicated by screeches and grunts. We should not ask whether any particular grunt is logically or factually true. At the other extreme is

[2]And it may be worth remarking that physics is doing quite nicely for itself.

this semantically ideal community, our ordinary communicative behaviour falling somewhere in between. If we use 'language' in the sense defined in chapter v then we are tempted to say that ordinarily we use something which is not quite a language, to ask what this something is and to reply that it is a "natural" language—something no one would expect to be logically precise. In view of the difficulty which would be encountered in trying to arrive at any systematic account of *natural languages* (in this sense) it seems to me to be preferable *not* to say that we ordinarily use something which is not quite a language, but to say instead that our ordinary communicative behaviour is not quite the use of a language. In *pure* pragmatics the fact that nobody quite uses a language will bother us no more than the fact that there are no perfect circles in nature or perfectly flat surfaces bothers the pure geometer.

And although the looseness of our ordinary discourse is of importance in a field like, say, propaganda analysis, *all the really interesting philosophical problems have to do with a semantically ideal community which exactly uses a language.* Such problems are "really interesting" because fully general. They are not engendered merely by the parochial locutions of either plain men or professors of philosophy in the English-speaking world. For example, since the publication of the White-Quine papers, there is a question as to the existence of a community (*qua* ideal) which uses a language for which the analytic-synthetic distinction holds.

It is here that we can take up the question of triviality raised above (p. 97). Earlier the fact that our general definition of language covers only languages of a single logical type led us to wonder if the definition of 'language' is not trivial. But suppose that in a burst of sophomoric enthusiasm we wished to tackle a very general (i.e., metaphysical) question like, "What general features must a world exhibit if it is to contain objects, and subjects capable of knowing those objects and describing them in a language?" (This seems to me to be an interesting question, an *a priori* question, and perhaps even answerable.) And suppose further that to attack this question we found that we required a general definition of 'language'. Then if we could get a fairly straightforward general definition we might reasonably congratulate ourselves rather than complain about the lack of logical variety among the languages covered by our definition. In other words, if there are important purposes for which something like D39 is required and for which D39 is adequate, then this circumstance constitutes a sufficient defence against the allegation of triviality.

The kind of idealization mentioned at the beginning of this section entails that pure pragmatics is not quite as simple as originally suggested. In laying down descriptive semiotic procedures, we do not take a man off the street and ask: How shall we go about discovering which language he uses? For the chances are that he does not exactly use a language at all. We should have to proceed in the opposite direction. We should *start with a language* and then ask: How would one set about using this language and by what signs would somebody else know that he was using it?

We have arrived at a vantage point from which we can now view more clearly the controversy over the analytic-synthetic distinction. In regard to the so-called problem of analyticity in natural languages we can object to the phrasing and yet concede the point. Most of the *responsiones* to White and Quine have taken the form of heaping contumely on natural languages (on what I should prefer to call 'ordinary communicative behaviour') and insisting that salvation lies with the precisely defined artificial language systems. This kind of reply may be essentially sound, but it is likely to be irritating, because we do not want merely to be told where salvation lies, we want a road map. If the semanticist is going to heap contumely on ordinary communicative behaviour, he might reasonably be expected to tell us how to correct the error of our ways and transform ourselves into a semantically ideal community. Supposing we were to decide to use one of the artificial languages, *so hold und schön und rein*, how would we set about doing it and how would somebody else know we were doing it? These are the questions that theoretical descriptive semiotic would have to deal with and any suitable definientia for FDP1–3 would have to supply answers.

§32. DESCRIPTIVE ANALYTICITY

As a final question, we may ask: How does the distinction between necessary and contingent truth now stand? We have a general definition of 'logically true' and we can be reasonably clear as to what we should want in the way of a full explication of logical truth. But there are still some puzzles connected with descriptive analyticity.

The descriptively analytic sentences (i.e., sentences containing one or more descriptive expressions essentially) fall into two classes. The first class contain those sentences which are true "by definition", e.g.,

(14)   All bachelors are unmarried.

The second class contain those descriptively analytic sentences which do not contain defined terms, for example,

(15)   If x is taller than y and y is taller than z then x is taller than z.
(16)   Red is between orange and purple.

I do not see any very grave problems over sentences of the first class. We have already lost interest in "natural" languages and I should not expect any major difficulties in the way of finding general requirements governing the introduction of defined terms into the so-called artificial languages. And Carnap (in *Synonymy*) has suggested what seem in principle to be satisfactory procedures for testing descriptive semiotic sentences like,

E_1 and E_1 are synonymous in the language used by P.

But with the second class of descriptively analytic sentences we have something else again. It has been suggested that we simply introduce meaning postulates to formalize the syntactical meaning of those primitive expressions which enter into descriptively analytic sentences.[3] The difficulty is this: Where do these meaning postulates come from? Do we just pull them out of the air? Of course, in constructing a calculus we pull primitive sentences out of the air. But there are rules for playing *that* game: the resulting calculus must be consistent and should preferably satisfy some sort of completeness requirement. What is wanted in the way of an explication of descriptive analyticity is a set of requirements, comparable to the completeness and consistency requirements for logic, to serve as rules to govern the game of pulling meaning postulates out of the air.

But of course we do not arbitrarily pull meaning postulates out of the air. They precipitate out of the used metalanguage and they do so in this way: Suppose we have a language L_5 for which the following are rules:

(1)   'rd' G-designates Red (in L_5),
(2)   'ornge' G-designates Orange,
(3)   'pple' G-designates Purple,
(4)   'Betw' G-designates Between.

Since 'Red is between orange and purple' is analytic in M, the statement, 'Betw(rd, ornge, pple)' has to be a meaning postulate of

[3] See Carnap, *Meaning Postulates.*

L_5; it precipitates out of the metalanguage in the sense that its necessity is a consequence of the necessity of its metalinguistic translation. But what shall and what shall not be allowed to precipitate into the object language as a meaning postulate?

The difficulty can be looked at in another way. The meanings of the logical primitives are specified by a listing of primitive sentences and deduction rules. Satisfaction of the consistency and completeness requirements assures us that our complex specification of meanings "fit together". The difficulty with primitive descriptive words like 'red' and 'taller than' is that their meanings are specified by designation rules and meaning postulates jointly. What is to tell us that we have not attributed too much or too little meaning to an expression as, in the case of a primitive logical sign, the satisfaction of the consistency and completeness requirements tells us when we have hit it just right? It is because *defined* descriptive expressions do not have designation rules that they raise no particular question.

And the rationale of type theory seems to me to be precisely this: Suppose we admit the sentence 'Hard(Brown)'. What are we to do with it? We should probably feel inclined to regard it as false and, moreover, as necessarily false. Then '∼Hard(Brown)' is necessarily true. But I can see no way of stating the meaning of 'Hard' and of 'Brown' in such a way that the truth of '∼Hard(Brown)' follows from the statement of meaning. In other words we really have no reason either to declare it true or to declare it false. Thus apart from the possibility of *arbitrarily* declaring this sentence to be true we have no alternative but to call it meaningless.

The difficulty mentioned above—that is, the difficulty of establishing the meaning of an expression by meaning postulates and designation rules jointly—suggests that there is something wrong with designation rules. Suppose we were to define a calculus K_1 in the following way: In K_1, '&' means *and*, '∨' means *or* and '∼' means *not*. Logicians would look upon our efforts as pretty feeble. Yet, with their designation rules, current semantic methods (including of course those of this book) are scarcely less crude. What we need to do is eviscerate the metalanguage of its descriptive expressions, at the same time dispensing with designation rules. It would only be possible to achieve this essential impoverishment of the metalanguage in secondary semantics, an offshoot of pure pragmatics. We have just about reached the limit of what can be accomplished in primary semantics.

Appendix: Cardinal Arithmetic

§1. DIFFICULTIES AND SUGGESTIONS

A general definition of 'mathematical superstructure' will not be given. But in view of the evident impossibility of introducing arithmetic into the languages of G by ordinary methods, new methods must be found and exhibited at least in the case of a specific language. A reduction of arithmetic to logic along logicistic lines is out of the question: our languages simply do not have the resources. And so we may stop to consider the motives behind the logicistic programme. One aim was to make clear the meanings of numerals in descriptive contexts. But this kind of clarification can be accomplished just as well by an axiom set as by explicit definition. The other motive was presumably the desire for ontological parsimony. Numbers are mysterious entities and if they can be conjured out of existence by defining numerical contexts with resources which do not commit us to an ontology of numbers, then so much the better from the standpoint of intellectual ease and comfort. But by the ontological criterion adopted in chapter IV there are no numbers anyway—they are pseudo-entities—and numbers do not have to be conjured out of existence by reduction. Thus we may, without compunction, abandon the whole reductionistic programme of *Principia Mathematica*.

A more specific difficulty is this: Suppose we want to say:

(1)   There are precisely five foolish virgins.

We do not use class expressions—not in our object languages, at any rate. And so (1) cannot be taken as ascribing a numerical property to the class of foolish virgins or assigning that class to a cardinal class. And even supposing the language recognizes the properties *foolishness* and *virginity* ('foolish' and 'virgin' being primitive), it does *not* recognize the conjunctive property of being both foolish and virgin. Therefore (1) cannot be taken as ascribing a numerical property to the property of being a foolish virgin or assigning it to a cardinal class. For there is no such property.

Therefore we shall have to reconcile ourselves to using numerals in descriptive sentences like (1) in places which are neither predicate nor argument places. We can do this because the numerals do not G-designate anything, even though they may appear in argument places of pure arithmetic statements and are replaceable by quantifiable variables. Numerical variables pseudo-range. We shall construct what will be called 'numerical operators' in analogy to the existential operators. Thus (1) would be expressed as:

(2)   (P5x)(x is foolish and x is virgin),

which is read as, "There are precisely five individuals which are foolish and virgin". When it comes to laying down axioms it will actually be more convenient to start with an operator '(5x)', which will mean, "There are at least five individuals x which are . . . ." This is in accord with the fact that numerals presumably have their origin with counting, and in counting the petals on a flower (for example), the "one, two, three . . ." can be taken as short for: "there is at least one petal, there are at least two petals, there are at least three petals . . . ."

The apparent difficulty which has been in the background all along and which inspired chapter IV has to do with our habitual ways of thinking about ontology. Speaking for myself, at any rate, I should say that in the beginning I would have taken it for granted that every entity is either an individual, a proposition, a property of an entity, a relation among entities, or a class or sequence of entities. The expressions by which an entity is designated may always appear in some argument place. Now leaving aside individuals, propositions, classes and sequences, and their designators, we should have it that a designative expression must "first" appear in a predicate place. It may also, if it is designative, appear "subsequently" in an argument place.[1] But we should think it odd if an expression in a connective place or operator place were treated as designative and allowed to appear elsewhere in an argument place. And the reason is that such an expression cannot possibly name a property or relation. We would regard '$\exists = \exists$' as downright silly. Nevertheless I propose to adopt this procedure with numerals. We shall have the numeral '5' appearing "first" in sentences like '(5x)(Fx)' (i.e., "There are at least five F's") and then "subsequently" in the sentence '5 = 5'.

There are at least two ways in which the incongruity could be resolved. We might take the view that we were simply mistaken in holding that all higher order entities must be properties of or relations among other entities. We might hold that numbers are an exotic kind of entity of an altogether different sort, their exotic character

---

[1]Quine would of course disagree, since he holds that although "foolishness" may conceivably name a property, "foolish" does not; and "foolish = foolish" would be ill-formed in his view.

being evidenced by the appearance of numerals in operator places. Or we might (as I have chosen to do and for reasons set out in chapter IV) remain loyal to our ontological prejudices and hold that there are no entities which are numbers, that numerals do not designate, *notwithstanding ineliminable quantification over numerical variables*. We admit a sentence like '5 = 5' in analogy to '∃ = ∃' and we admit the existential quantification, '(∃n)($n = 5$)' and '(∃n)[(Pnx)(Fx) & (Pnx)(Gx)]', and we treat all this as a convenient, ontologically non-significant symbolic mumbo-jumbo, justified because we get a system which works, which gives us what we want. It might be added that I do not regard all philosophy as the business of finding expedient methods of symbolic manipulation, justified by a kind of superficial adequacy and absence of flat inconsistency. But it does seem to me that if a discipline (here, arithmetic) *can* be regarded as just a clever kind of symbolic mumbo-jumbo, then we may quite properly so regard it, precisely in order to put it to one side and enjoy an uncluttered field in which to attack the real ontology of proto-facts (as distinct from the pseudo-ontology generated by symbolism).

So much for the philosophy of mathematics. Now for the mathematics. It is worth mentioning that the method which follows is, in effect, a combination of logicistic and formalistic approaches. We shall try to enjoy the best of both worlds.

§2. A SAMPLE MATHEMATICAL SUPERSTRUCTURE IN G

We can suppose that the language L_2, defined in chapter III (§8), is supplemented (to yield L_3) in a manner specified by the following rules:

1. 'n', 'm' etc. are numerical variables (of L_3, always).
2. '1' is a numeral (i.e., a numerical constant).
3. There is a sign 'Σ' such that if E is a numerical expression (constant or variable) then $\Sigma'E$ (more accurately, $\mathscr{A}'('\Sigma','"', E)$) is a numerical expression.

('Σ' is to be read as "succeeds". The inverted apostrophe indicates a Russellian descriptive phrase, so that '$\Sigma'n$' would be defined in the manner of *PM* *30.01 as '($\imath m)\Sigma(m,n)$', with the inverted iota defined in the usual way. It follows that 'Σ' is a two-place predicate taking numerical expressions as arguments.)

4. No expression is a numerical expression unless it so qualifies under rules 1–3.

5. 'Φ' is a one-place predicate taking numerical expressions as arguments.

(We shall use 'N', 'N_1', 'N_j' as restricted metalinguistic variables ranging over just the numerical expressions of L_3, in the manner suggested in §18.)

6. E is a numerical operator of L_3 if and only if there is a variable v from the elementary part of L_3 and a numerical expression N such that $E = Nv$.

7. E is a numerical sentence of L_3 if and only if
    (a) E is of the form $N_1 = N_1$
or (b) there is a numerical operator Nv and a sentence S (open or closed) from the elementary part of L_3 such that $E = (Nv)S$.

For the sake of brevity I shall assume without giving explicit rules, that numerical sentences can be compounded with connectives to yield complex numerical sentences and that they may be prefixed with quantifiers containing numerical variables. I shall also assume that quantification over numerical variables is subject to the usual rules of quantificational logic and that the identity sign in numerical statements has its usual syntactical properties.

In laying down axioms to establish the logical properties of the numerical operators it will be convenient to dispense with 'Σ' by means of the following definition:

MD1. $n' =_{dt} \Sigma'n.$

The point of introducing 'Σ' as primitive and then defining "'" is to avoid a *tacit* assumption of the uniqueness of the successor of a number (as with Peano), this assumption being made a little more explicitly by taking "'" as primitive and characterizing it as a functor expression. At any rate I prefer the still more explicit manœuvre of adopting an axiom, MAx3.

In the following, 'F' and 'Φ' are used as schematic letters. By so using them we are able to express what in the metalanguage we get at with the phrase "for all contexts". We shall require a rule of substitution, to be given shortly.

MAx1. $(1x)(Fx) \equiv (\exists x)(Fx).$

("There is at least one individual which is F if and only if . . . .")

MAx2. $(n'x)(Fx) \equiv (\exists y)[Fy \ \& \ (nx)(x \neq y \ \& \ Fx)].$

("There are at least n' F's if and only if there is at least one F such that there are at least n *other* F's.") Axioms 1 and 2 provide an enumerative and recursive contextual definition of numerals in operator places. We now need axioms which will guarantee the existence and uniqueness of successors and the uniqueness of predecessors (if any).

MAx3. E!Σ'n.
MAx4. $n' = m' \supset n = m$.

And we shall need the induction axiom to guarantee that only pseudo-entities in the posterity of 1 are values of the variable 'n'.

MAx5. $\Phi 1 \supset [(n)(\Phi n \supset \Phi n') \supset (n)(\Phi n)]$.

Deduction Rule.

I shall state the rule of substitution informally:

Given a *provable* sentence containing one or more occurrences of 'F' with an individual expression—perhaps with different individual expressions in different occurrences—then the partial sentence 'Fx' may be replaced throughout by any other partial sentence containing 'x' freely, provided that all partial sentences containing 'F' are replaced by something "appropriate", that is, if, for example, 'Fx' is replaced by '$Fx \& x \neq z$', then 'Fy' must be replaced by '$Fy \& y \neq z$'. The schematic letter 'Φ' is subject to a similar rule, as is also the two-place schematic letter 'R', which takes individual expressions as arguments. The rule of substitution is essentially that given by Quine in §25 of his *Methods* (to which the reader is referred) except that here two-place predicate schemata may be substituted for one-place predicate letters. It is as if the other variable (e.g., 'z' in '$Fx \& x \neq z$') were "held constant" during the substitution.

Substitution for 'Φ' is necessary in using MAx5 to perform mathematical induction. It is necessary in some inductions to substitute for 'F'. These are the cases where the hypothesis of the induction would not normally be saying what we want it to say to complete the induction step, and it must therefore be taken as having the same force as "For all contexts of 'x' . . .".

Of course we shall have standard number theoretic definitions of the defined numerals and of the operations of addition and multiplication, and of the relation *greater than*, with the minor changes required by the fact that our number system starts from 1, not from 0.

MD2₂. $2 =_{df} 1'$.   MD2₃. $3 =_{df} 2'$ etc.

MD3. $n + 1 =_{df} n'$.
$\qquad n + m' =_{df} (n + m)'$.

MD4. $n.1 =_{df} n$.
$\qquad n.m' =_{df} n.m + n$.

MD5. $n > m =_{df} (\exists k)(m + k = n)$.

We shall have, in addition, definitions of the secondary numerical operators:

MD6. $(Mnx)(Fx) =_{df} \sim(n'x)(Fx)$.

("There are at most n individuals which are F means that it is not the case that there are at least n' individuals which are F.")

MD7. $(Pnx)(Fx) =_{df} (nx)(Fx) \ \& \ (Mnx)(Fx)$.

("There are precisely n F's means that there are at least n F's and there are at most n F's.") All three operators '(nx)', '(Mnx)' and '(Pnx)' have the effect of binding the operator variable in its occurrences within the scope of that operator.

§3. ELEMENTARY THEOREMS

Limitations of space make it impossible to include more than a few of the more difficult or characteristic proofs of the fifty theorems to be listed in this and the next two sections. Proofs of the early theorems are quite straightforward.

Th1. $(P1x)(x = y)$.
$\qquad$ Expand by MD7, MD6, MAx2 and MAx1 and prove by elementary logic.
Th2. $n \neq 1 \supset (\exists m)(m' = n)$.
$\qquad$ From MAx5.
Th3. $\sim(n' = 1)$.

"1 is not the successor of any number." From Theorems 1 and 2 by *reductio ad absurdum*.

Clearly, Axioms 3, 4, and 5 together with Theorem 3 supply sufficient foundations for pure cardinal arithmetic along familiar lines. We may assume without statement here the usual number-theoretic proofs for the associative, commutative, and distributive laws of addition and multiplication, and for such theorems as '$n' + m = n + m''$'. Whenever these are to be invoked, we shall simply cite 'N.T.' (for "Number Theory"). All the subsequent theorems will be concerned immediately or ultimately with the use of numerals in descriptive contexts. Theorems 4–10 are offered in preparation for Theorem 11.

Th4. $n > m \supset (n = m' \lor n > m')$.
Th5. $m > n \supset m' > n$.
Th6. $n = 1 \lor n > 1$.
Cor. $n = 1 \lor n > 1 \lor 1 > n$.
Th7. $n = m \lor n > m \lor m > n$.

By induction, with Theorem 6, Cor. as basis. The induction step is proved from Theorems 4 and 5.

Cor. $n \neq m \supset (n > m \lor m > n)$.
Th8. $((m + k)x)(Fx) \supset (m'x) Fx)$
      By cases: $k = 1$ or else $k > 1$.
Th9. $n > m \supset [(nx)(Fx) \supset \sim(Mmx)(Fx)]$.
      From Theorem 8, MD5, and MD6.
Th10. $m > n \supset [(Mnx)(Fx) \supset \sim(mx)(Fx)]$.
      From Theorem 9.
Th11. $n \neq m \supset [(Pnx)(Fx) \supset \sim(Pmx)(Fx)]$.
      From Theorem 7, Cor. and Theorems 9 and 10.

If I have (precisely) four dogs and four cats, it follows quite directly that I have the same number of dogs as cats. But if I have three dogs and five cats it follows, not so directly, but is assured by Theorem 11, that it is not the case that I have the same number of dogs as cats.

§4. THEOREMS FOR ADDITION

Apart from Theorem 27, which is of some intrinsic interest, all the theorems of this section serve as lemmas for the proof of Theorem 35.

Th12. $(x)(Fx \supset Gx) \supset [(1x)(Fx) \supset (1x)(Gx)]$.
      From MAx1 and elementary logic.
Th13. $(x)(Fx \supset Gx) \supset [(nx)(Fx) \supset (nx)(Gx)]$.

By induction with Theorem 12 as basis. In the induction step the hypothesis is reiterated and varied by replacing 'Fx' and 'Gx' by '$x \neq y \,\&\, Fx$' and '$x \neq y \,\&\, Gx$' respectively. Theorem 13 is rather useful since it allows us, in analogy to existence elimination deductions,

deductions of the following general form (for which Theorem 13 will be cited):

$$(nx)(Fx)$$

$$\begin{array}{l} \overline{Fx} \qquad\qquad \text{Hypoth.} \\ \cdots \\ \cdots \\ Gx \end{array}$$

$$(nx)(Gx).$$

Th14. $(x)(Fx \supset Gx) \supset [(Mnx)(Gx) \supset (Mnx)(Fx)]$.
From Theorem 13.

Th15. $A \supset [(nx)(Fx) \supset (nx)(Fx \,\&\, A)]$. (No free '$x$' in '$A$'.)
From Theorem 13.

Th16. $(nx)(Fx) \supset (\exists x)(Fx)$.

Th17. $(nx)(x \neq y \,\&\, Fx) \supset (nx)(Fx)$.
From Theorem 13.

Th18. $(n'x)(Fx) \supset (nx)(Fx)$.
From MAx2 and Theorem 17.

Th19. $(Mnx)(Fx) \supset (Mn'x)(Fx)$.
From Theorem 18.

Th20. $(Mnx)(Fx) \supset (Mnx)(x \neq y \,\&\, Fx)$.
From Theorem 14.

Th21. $Fy \supset [(nx)(x \neq y \,\&\, Fx) \supset (n'x)(Fx)]$.
Importation, existential generalization, MAx2.

Th22. $Fy \supset [(Mn'x)(Fx) \supset (Mnx)(x \neq y \,\&\, Fx)]$.
From Theorem 21.

Th23. $Fz \supset [(1'x)(Fx) \supset (1x)(x \neq z \,\&\, Fx)]$.
Expand the operators and prove by elementary logic.

Th24. $Fz \supset [(n'x)(Fx) \supset (nx)(x \neq z \,\&\, Fx)]$.
By induction with Theorem 23 as basis.

Th25. $(n'x)(Fx) \supset (nx)(x \neq z \,\&\, Fx)$.
By cases: either Fz, in which case the theorem follows by Theorem 24; or else $\sim Fz$, in which case the theorem follows by Theorems 13 and 18.

Th26. $(Mnx)(x \neq y \,\&\, Fx) \supset (Mn'x)(Fx)$.
From Theorem 25.

Th27. $(Pn'x)(Fx) \equiv (\exists y)[Fy \,\&\, (Pnx)(x \neq y \,\&\, Fx)]$.
From MD7, MAx2, Theorems 22, 21, and 26.

Th28. $(M1x)(Fx) \equiv (y)(z)[Fy \supset (Fz \supset y = z)]$.
From MD6 and elementary logic.

Th29. $(M1x)(Fx) \supset [((1 + 1)x)(Fx \lor Gx) \supset (1x)(Gx)]$.

From Theorem 28 and elementary logic.

Th30. $(Mnx)(Fx) \supset [((n + 1)x)(Fx \lor Gx) \supset (1x)(Gx)]$.

Prove by induction with Theorem 29 as basis. Assume the theorem holds (is provable) for n and prove for n'. The induction hypothesis is to be taken as reiterated after line (11) and then subjected to the rule of substitution, 'Fx' and 'Gx' being replaced by '$x \neq y$ & Fx' and '$x \neq y$ & Gx' respectively.[2]

(1)	$(Mn'x)(Fx)$	Hypoth.
(2)	$((n' + 1)x)(Fx \lor Gx)$ (i.e., $((n + 1)'x) \ldots$)	Hypoth.
(3)	$(\exists y)\{(Fy \lor Gy)$ & $((n + 1)x)[(x \neq y$ & $Fx)$ $\lor (x \neq y$ & $Gx)]\}$	(2), MAx2.
(4a)	y $(Fy \lor Gy)$ &	
(4b)	$((n + 1)x)[(x \neq y$ & $Fx) \lor (x \neq y$ & $Gx)]$	Hypoth.
(5)	$Gy \lor \sim Gy$	
(6)	Gy	Hypoth.
(7)	$(\exists x)(Gx)$	$\exists$-intro, (6).
(8)	$(1x)(Gx)$	(7), MAx1.
(9)	$\sim Gy$	
(10)	Fy	(4a), (9).
(11)	$(Mnx)(x \neq y$ & $Fx)$	(10), (1), Th22.
(12)	$(1x)(x \neq y$ & $Gx)$	(11), (4b), Ind. Hyp. (Subst.).
(13)	$(1x)(Gx)$	(12), Th17.
(14)	$(1x)(Gx)$	$\lor$-elim., (5), (6)–(8), (9)–(13).
(15)	$(1x)(Gx)$	$\exists$-elim., (3), (4)–(14).
(16)	$(Mn'x)(Fx) \supset [((n' + 1)x)(Fx \lor Gx) \supset (1x)(Gx)]$	
		$\supset$-intro., (2)–(15), (1)–(15).

The theorem holds for n' if it holds for n. Hence the theorem.

Th31. $(Mnx)(Fx) \supset [((n + m)x)(Fx \lor Gx) \supset (mx)(Gx)]$.

Prove by induction on m, with Theorem 30 as basis. At line (6) the induction hypothesis is reiterated and substitutions made as in the proof of Theorem 30. It is also to be taken as reiterated at line (32) and different substitutions made as called for.

---

[2] The style of proof here has been adapted from F. B. Fitch, *Symbolic Logic*, and S. C. Kleene, *Introduction to Metamathematics*.

(1)	$(Mnx)(Fx)$	Hypoth.
(2)	$((n + m')x)(Fx \lor Gx)$	Hypoth.
(3)	$(\exists y)\{(Fy \lor Gy) \,\&\, ((n + m)x)[x \neq y \,\&\, (Fx \lor Gx)]\}$	
		(2), N.T., MAx2.
(4a)	$y \quad (Fy \lor Gy) \,\&\,$	
(4b)	$\qquad ((n + m)x)[x \neq y \,\&\, (Fx \lor Gx)]$	Hypoth.
(5)	$(Mnx)(x \neq y \,\&\, Fx)$	(1), Th20.
(6)	$(mx)(x \neq y \,\&\, Gx)$	(5), (4b), Ind. Hyp. (Subst.).
(7)	$Gy \lor \sim Gy$	
(8)	Gy	Hypoth.
(9)	$(m'x)(Gx)$	(8), (6), Th21.
(10)	$\sim Gy$	Hypoth.
(11)	$n = 1 \lor n \neq 1$	
(12)	$n = 1$	Hypoth.
(13)	$(M1x)(Fx)$	(1), (12).
(14)	$((1 + m)x)[x \neq y \,\&\, (Fx \lor Gx)]$	(4b), (12).
(15a)	$x \quad x \neq y \,\&\,$	
(15b)	$\qquad (Fx \lor Gx)$	Hypoth.
(16)	Fy	(4a), (10).
(17)	$\sim Fx$	(13), (16), (15a), Th28.
(18)	Gx	(15b), (17).
(19)	$((1 + m)x)(Gx)$	(14), (15)–(18), Th13.
(20)	$(m'x)(Gx)$	(19), N.T.
(21)	$n \neq 1$	Hypoth.
(22)	Let $p' = n$	Th2.
(23)	$(\exists z)(z \neq y \,\&\, Gz)$	(6), Th16.
(24)	$z \quad z \neq y \,\&\, Gz$	Hypoth.
(25)	$z \neq y \,\&\, (Fz \lor Gz)$	$\lor$-intro., (24).
(26)	$((p' + m)x)[x \neq y \,\&\, (Fx \lor Gx)]$	(4b), (22).
(27)	$((p + m)x)[x \neq z \,\&\, x \neq y \,\&\, (Fx \lor Gx)]$	
		(26), N.T., Th25.
(28)	$(Mp'x)(Fx)$	(1), (22).
(29)	Fy	(4a), (10).
(30)	$(Mpx)(x \neq y \,\&\, Fx)$	(29), (28), Th22.
(31)	$(Mpx)(x \neq z \,\&\, x \neq y \,\&\, Fx)$	(30), Th20.
(32)	$(mx)(x \neq z \,\&\, x \neq y \,\&\, Gx)$	
		(31), (27), Ind. Hypoth. (Subst.).
(33)	$(mx)(x \neq z \,\&\, Gx)$	(32), Th17.
(34)	$Gz \,\&\, (mx)(x \neq z \,\&\, Gx)$	(24,) (33).
(35)	$(m'x)(Gx)$	(34), Th21.
(36)	$(m'x)(Gx)$	$\exists$-elim., (23), (24)–(35).
(37)	$(m'x)(Gx)$	$\lor$-elim., (11), (12)–(20), (21)–(36).
(38)	$(m'x)(Gx)$	$\lor$-elim., (7), (8)–(9), (10)–(37).
(39)	$(m'x)(Gx)$	$\exists$-elim., (3), (4)–(38).
(40)	$(Mnx)(Fx) \supset [((n + m')x)(Fx \lor Gx) \supset (m'x)(Gx)]$	
		$\supset$-intro., (2)–(39), (1)–(39).

The theorem holds for m' if it holds for m. Hence the theorem.

Th32. $(Mnx)(Fx) \supset [(Mnx)(Gx) \supset (M(n + m)x)(Fx \lor Gx)]$.
From Theorem 31.

Th33. $(x)(Fx \supset {\sim}Gx) \supset (1x)(Fx) \supset (mx)(Gx) \supset$
$$((1 + m)x) (Fx \lor Gx).$$
From Theorem 13. In this and in subsequent cases where parentheses are omitted, grouping is from the right.

Th34. $(x)(Fx \supset {\sim}Gx) \supset (nx)(Fx) \supset (mx)(Gx) \supset$
$$((n + m)x)(Fx \lor Gx).$$
By induction, with Theorem 33 as basis, Theorems 13 and 25.

Th35. $(x)(Fx \supset {\sim}Gx) \supset (Pnx)(Fx) \supset (Pmx)(Gx) \supset$
$$(P(n + m)x) (Fx \lor Gx).$$
From Theorems 32 and 34.

Theorem 35 assures me that if I have (precisely) three dogs and four cats, then I have seven dogs-or-cats.

§5. THEOREMS FOR MULTIPLICATION

Again we are aiming at the proof of a particular theorem, Theorem 50, and all the other theorems are preliminary lemmas. In the following, 'R' will be used as a two-place schematic letter, subject to the rule of substitution.

Th36. $((1 + m)x)(Fx) \supset (mx)(Fx)$.
From Theorem 18 and number theory.
Th37. $((n + m)x)(Fx) \supset (mx)(Fx)$.
By induction on n, with Theorem 36 as basis.
Th38. $(M1x)(Rzx) \supset y \neq v \supset ({\sim}Rzy \lor {\sim}Rzv)$.
From Theorem 28.
Th39. $(y)[(M1x)(Rxy)] \supset Rxy \supset Rzv \supset x \neq z \supset y \neq v$.
From Theorem 28.
Th40. $(M1x)(Rzx) \supset ((1 + 1)y)(\exists x)(Fx \ \& \ Rxy) \supset$
$$(1y)(\exists x)(x \neq z \ \& \ Fx \ \& \ Rxy).$$
This theorem is proved by a method similar to but simpler than that used in proving the induction step in Theorem 41.

Th41. $(M1x)(Rzx) \supset ((1 + m)y)(\exists x)(Fx \ \& \ Rxy) \supset$
$$(my)(\exists x)(x \neq z \ \& \ Fx \ \& \ Rxy).$$

Prove by induction with Theorem 40 as basis. The induction hypothesis is to be reiterated after line (16) and 'Rzx' replaced by 'Rzx & $x \neq y$'. The hypothesis also has to be relettered.

(1) $(\mathrm{M}1x)(Rzx)$ Hypoth.

(2) $((1 + m')y)(\exists x)(Fx \& Rxy)$ (i.e., $(m''y)(\ldots)$)   Hypoth.

(3) $(\exists v)(\exists w)[Fw \& Rwv \& (\exists y)\{y \neq v \& (\exists x)(Fx \& Rxy) \&$
         $(mu)[u \neq y \& u \neq v \& (\exists x)(Fx \& Rxu)]\}]$ (2), MAx2.

(4) $(\exists v)(\exists w)(\exists y)(\exists x)[Fw \& Rwv \& y \neq v \& Fx \& Rxy \&$
         $(mu)(\ldots \text{etc.})]$ (3).

(5) v $Fw \& Rwv \& y \neq v \& Fx \& Rxy \& (mu)(\ldots \text{etc.})$ Hypoth.

(6) w $\sim Rzy \lor \sim Rzv$ (1), (5), Th38.

(7) y $x \neq z \lor w \neq z$ (5), (6).

(8) x $x \neq z$

(9) $x \neq z \& Fx \& Rxy$ (8), (5).

(10) $(\exists x)(x \neq z \& Fx \& Rxy)$ $\exists$-intro., (9).

(11) $Fw \& Rwv \& v \neq y \& (mu)(\ldots \text{etc.})$ (5).

(12) $v \neq y \& (\exists x)(Fx \& Rxv) \& (mu)(\ldots \text{etc.})$ $\exists$-intro., (11).

(13) $(m'u)[u \neq y \& (\exists x)(Fx \& Rxu)]$ (12), Th21.

(14) $((1 + m)u)(\exists x)(Fx \& Rxu \& u \neq y)$ N.T., Import.

(15) $(\mathrm{M}1x)(Rzx \& x \neq y)$ (1), Th20.

(16) $(mu)(\exists x)(x \neq z \& Fx \& Rxu \& u \neq y)$
                       (15), (14), Ind. Hyp.

(17) $(m'y)(\exists x)(x \neq z \& Fx \& Rxy)$ (10), (16), Th21.

(18) $w \neq z$ Hypoth.
      Similarly

(19) $(m'y)(\exists x)(x \neq z \& Fx \& Rxy)$ $\lor$-elim., (7), (8)–(17), (18)–.

(20) $(m'y)(\exists x)(x \neq z \& Fx \& Rxy)$ $\exists$-elim., (4), (5)–(19).

(21) $(\mathrm{M}1x)(Rzx) \supset ((1 + m')y)(\exists x)(Fx \& Rxy) \supset (m'y)(\exists x)(x \neq z$
     $\& Fx \& Rxy)$ $\supset$-intro., (2)–(20), (1)–(20).

Hence the theorem.

Th42. $(\mathrm{M}nx)(Rzx) \supset ((n + m)y)(\exists x)(Fx \& Rxy) \supset$
                        $(my)(\exists x)(x \neq z \& Fx \& Rxy)$.

By induction on n, with Theorem 41 as basis. Prove the step by cases: either $(\exists u)(Rzu)$, in which case the step follows by Theorems 22, 25, and 17; or else $\sim(\exists u)(Rzu)$, in which case the step follows by Theorem 13 and 19.

Th43. $(y)[(\mathrm{M}1x)(Rxy)] \supset Fz \supset (1y)(Rzy) \supset (my)(\exists x)(x \neq z \& Fx \&$
             $Rxy) \supset ((1 + m)y)(\exists x)(Fx \& Rxy)$.

From Theorem 39.

Th44. $(y)[(\text{M}1x)(Rxy)] \supset Fz \supset (ny)(Rzy) \supset (my)(\exists x)(x \neq z$ & Fx
& $Rxy) \supset ((n+m)y)(\exists x)(Fx$ & $Rxy)$.

By induction on n, with Theorem 43 as basis. Theorem 14.

Th45. $(x)[Fx \supset (\text{M}ny)(Rxy)] \supset ((n.1)'y)(\exists x)(Fx$ & $Rxy) \supset$
$$(1'x)(Fx).$$

From Theorems 16, 28, and 13.

Th46. $(x)[Fx \supset (\text{M}ny)(Rxy)] \supset ((\text{n.m})'y)(\exists x)(Fx$ & $Rxy) \supset$
$$(m'x)(Fx).$$

Prove by induction on m, with Theorem 45 as basis. The induction hypothesis is to be reiterated at line (9) and varied by the replacement of 'Fx' by '$x \neq z$ & Fx'.

(1) $\quad (x)[Fx \supset (\text{M}ny)(Rxy)]$ — Hypoth.

(2) $\quad ((n.m')'y)(\exists x)(Fx$ & $Rxy)$ — Hypoth.

(3) $\quad (\exists w)(\exists z)(Fz$ & $Rzw)$ — (2), Th16, reletter.

(4) $w \quad Fz$ & Rzw — Hypoth.

(5) $z \quad (\text{M}ny)(Rzy)$ — (4), (1).

(6) $\quad ((n+(n.m)')y)(\exists x)(Fx$ & $Rxy)$ — (2), N.T.

(7) $\quad ((n.m)'y)(\exists x)(x \neq z$ & Fx & $Rxy)$ — (5), (6), Th42.

(8) $\quad (x)[(x \neq z$ & $Fx) \supset (\text{M}ny)(Rxy)]$ — (1).

(9) $\quad (m'x)(x \neq z$ & $Fx)$ — (8), (7), Ind. Hyp.

(10) $\quad Fz$ & $(m'x)(x \neq z$ & $Fx)$ — (4), (9).

(11) $\quad (\exists z)[Fz$ & $(m'x)(x \neq z$ & $Fx)]$ — $\exists$-elim., (3), (4)–(10).

(12) $\quad (m''x)(Fx)$ — (11), MAx2.

(13) $(x)[Fx \supset (\text{M}ny)(Rxy)] \supset ((n.m')'y)(\exists x)(Fx$ & $Rxy) \supset$
$(m''x)(Fx)$ — $\supset$-intro., (2)–(12), (1)–(12).

Hence the theorem.

Th47. $(x)[Fx \supset (\text{M}ny)(Rxy)] \supset (\text{M}mx)(Fx) \supset$
$$(\text{M}(n.m)y)(\exists x)(Fx$ & $Rxy).$$

Directly from Theorem 46, by contraposition of the last conditional and definition of 'M'.

Th48. $(y)[(\text{M}1x)(Rxy)] \supset (x)[Fx \supset (ny)(Rxy)] \supset (1x)(Fx) \supset$
$$((n.1)y)(\exists x)(Fx$ & $Rxy).$$

A simple proof using Theorem 13.

Th49. $(y)[(\text{M}1x)(Rxy)] \supset (x)[Fx \supset (ny)(Rxy)] \supset (my)(Fx) \supset$
$$((n.m)y)(\exists x)(Fx$ & $Rxy).$$

By induction on m, with Theorem 48 as basis. Theorem 44.

Th50. $(y)[(\text{M}1x)(Rxy)] \supset (x)[Fx \supset (Pny)(Rxy)] \supset (Pmx)(Fx) \supset$
$$(P(n.m)y)(\exists x)(Fx$ & $Rxy).$$

Quite directly from Theorems 47 and 49.

From Theorem 50 it follows that if I have seven cats and each of my cats has seven kittens of her own, then I have forty-nine kittens. We shall stop here.

Two observations may be offered in conclusion. In virtue of the fact that in descriptive sentences numerals stand, not in predicate or argument places, but in operator places, the mathematical superstructure stands rather to one side of the elementary portion of the language, and once in it, we enjoy very great freedom. There is no objection to constructing expressions for classes of numbers (i.e., classes of pseudo-entities), and expressions for properties of numbers, which expressions may be value expressions of the appropriate variables. Moreover, we may adopt any adequate device we please for avoiding the antinomies.

In the second place, although this system of cardinal arithmetic has a certain *ad hoc* or made-to-order quality about it, it can lay claim to some intrinsic interest apart from its connection with the definition of "language". It shares with formalism the advantage of getting along without an axiom of infinity and it shares with logicism the advantage of providing a clarification of descriptive arithmetic sentences like "There are nine planets". Its chief shortcoming—assuming the system to be not inconsistent—lies in the fact that although it is clearly adequate for pure cardinal arithmetic, it is not so clear that it is fully adequate for all descriptive arithmetic. But the possibility of giving proofs of the important theorems for addition and multiplication (Theorems 35 and 50) provides at least a presumption that it is adequate.

Bibliography

AMBROSE, ALICE. (*Inadequacy*) "The Problem of Linguistic Inadequacy," in Max Black (ed.), *Philosophical Analysis*. Ithaca, Cornell University Press, 1950, pp. 15–37.

CARNAP, RUDOLF. (*Ontology*) "Empiricism, Semantics and Ontology," *Revue Internationale de Philosophie*, vol. IV (1950), pp. 20–40. Reprinted in Linsky.

—— (*Formalization*) *Formalization of Logic*. Studies in Semantics, vol. II, Cambridge, Mass., Harvard University Press, 1943.

—— (*Foundations L & M*) "Foundations of Logic and Mathematics," *International Encyclopedia of Unified Science*, vol. I, no. 3, Chicago, University of Chicago Press, 1939.

—— (*Semantics*) *Introduction to Semantics*, Studies in Semantics, vol. I, Cambridge, Mass., Harvard University Press, 1942.

—— (*Probability*) *Logical Foundations of Probability*, Chicago, University of Chicago Press, 1950.

—— (*Syntax*) *The Logical Syntax of Language*, New York, Harcourt Brace, and London, Kegan Paul, 1937.

—— (*M & N*) *Meaning and Necessity*, Chicago, University of Chicago Press, 1947.

—— (*Synonymy*) "Meaning and Synonymy in Natural Languages," *Philosophical Studies*, vol. VI (1955), pp. 33–47.

—— "Meaning Postulates," *Philosophical Studies*, vol. III (1952), pp. 65–73.

—— (*Belief*) "On Belief Sentences: Reply to Alonzo Church," in Margaret Macdonald (ed.), *Analysis*, pp. 128–31.

CHURCH, ALONZO. (*Rev. Carnap*) "Carnap's Introduction to Semantics," *Philosophical Review*, vol. LII (1943), pp. 298–304.

—— (*Abstract Entities*) "The Need for Abstract Entities in Semantic Analysis," *Proceedings of the American Academy of Arts and Sciences*, vol. LXXX (1951), pp. 100–12.

—— (*Assertion*) "On Carnap's Analysis of Statements of Assertion and Belief," *Analysis*, vol. X (1950), pp. 97–9. Reprinted in Margaret Macdonald (ed.), *Analysis*, pp. 125–7.

FEIGL, HERBERT and SELLARS, WILFRID (eds.). *Readings in Philosophical Analysis*, New York, Appleton-Century-Crofts, Inc., 1949.

FITCH, F. B. (*Intuitionistic*) "Intuitionistic Modal Logic with Quantifiers," *Portugaliae Mathematica*, vol. VII (1948), pp. 113–18.

—— *Symbolic Logic: An Introduction*, New York, Ronald Press, 1952.

GÖDEL, KURT. "Ueber formal unentscheidbare Sätze der Principia Mathematica und verwandter Systeme," *Monatshefte für Mathematik und Physik*, vol. XXXVIII (1931), pp. 173–98.

GOODMAN, NELSON. (*Counterfactuals*) "The Problem of Counterfactual Conditionals," *Journal of Philosophy*, vol. XLIV (1947), pp. 113–28. Reprinted in Linsky.

GOODMAN, NELSON and QUINE, W. V. (*Steps*) "Steps towards a Constructive Nominalism," *Journal of Symbolic Logic*, vol. XII (1947), pp. 105–22.

HEMPEL, CARL G. (*Concept Formation*) "Fundamentals of Concept Formation in Empirical Science," *International Encyclopedia of Unified Science*, vol. II, no. 7, Chicago, University of Chicago Press, 1952.

KLEENE, S. C. *Introduction to Metamathematics*, Amsterdam, North-Holland Publishing Co., and Groningen, P. Noordhoff; New York and Toronto, D. van Nostrand Co., 1952.

LINSKY, LEONARD (ed.). *Semantics and the Philosophy of Language*, Urbana, University of Illinois Press, 1952.

MACDONALD, MARGARET (ed.). (*Analysis*) *Philosophy and Analysis*, Oxford, Blackwell, 1954.

MARTIN, R. M. (*Concatenation*) "On Inscriptions and Concatenation," *Philosophy and Phenomenological Research*, vol. XII (1951–52), pp. 418–21.

NELSON, E. J. (*Contradiction*) "Contradiction and the Presupposition of Existence," *Mind*, vol. LV (1946), pp. 319–27.

OGDEN, C. K. and RICHARDS I. A. (*Meaning*) *The Meaning of Meaning*, New York, Harcourt Brace and London, Kegan Paul, 1923.

QUINE, W. V. (*Designation*) "Designation and Existence," *Journal of Philosophy*, vol. XXXVI (1939), pp. 701–9. Reprinted in Feigl and Sellars.

——— (*LPV*) *From a Logical Point of View*, Cambridge, Harvard University Press, 1953.

——— (*ML*) *Mathematical Logic* (1st ed.), Cambridge, Harvard University Press, 1940.

——— (*Methods*) *Methods of Logic*, New York, Henry Holt, 1950.

——— (*Notes*) "Notes on Existence and Necessity," *Journal of Philosophy*, vol. XL (1943), pp. 113–27. Reprinted in Linsky.

——— (*On What*) "On What There Is," *Review of Metaphysics*, vol. II (1948–49), pp. 21–38. Reprinted in Linsky.

——— (*Modal Logic*) "The Problem of Interpreting Modal Logic," *Journal of Symbolic Logic*, vol. XII (1947), pp. 43–8.

——— (*Rev. Nelson*) A review of E. J. Nelson's "Contradiction and the Presupposition of Existence," *Journal of Symbolic Logic*, vol. XII (1947), pp. 52–5.

——— (*Rev. Barcan*) A review of Ruth C. Barcan's "The Identity of Individuals in a Strict Functional Calculus of Second Order," *Journal of Symbolic Logic*, vol. XII (1947), pp. 95–6.

——— (*Objects*) "Speaking of Objects," Presidential Address, *Proceedings and Addresses of the American Philosophical Association*, vol. XXXI (1957–8), pp. 5–22.

——— (*Dogmas*) "Two Dogmas of Empiricism," *Philosophical Review*, vol. LX (1951), pp. 20–43. Reprinted, with changes, in *LPV*.

RAMSEY, F. P. (*Foundations*) *The Foundations of Mathematics and other Logical Essays*, London, Kegan Paul, 1931.

RUSSELL, BERTRAND. (*Math. Phil.*) *Introduction to Mathematical Philosophy*, London, Allen and Unwin, 1919.

RUSSELL, BERTRAND and WHITEHEAD, A. N. See WHITEHEAD, A. N. and RUSSELL, BERTRAND.

RYLE, GILBERT. *The Concept of Mind*, London, Hutchinson's University Library, 1949.

SELLARS, WILFRID. (*Empiricism*) "Empiricism and the Philosophy of Mind," in Feigl, Herbert and Scriven, Michael (eds.), *The Foundations of Science and the Concepts of Psychology and Psychoanalysis*, *Minnesota Studies in the Philosophy of Sciences*, vol. I (1956), pp. 253–329.

——— (*Identity*) "The Identity of Linguistic Expressions and the Paradox of Analysis," *Philosophical Studies*, vol. I (1950), pp. 24–31.

——— (*Quotes*) "Quotation Marks, Sentences and Propositions," *Philosophy and Phenomenological Research*, vol. X (1950), pp. 515–25.

——— (*RNWW*) "Realism and the New Way of Words," *Philosophy and Phenomenological Research*, vol. VIII (1948), pp. 601–34.

SMULLYAN, ARTHUR FRANCIS. (*Modality*) "Modality and Description," *Journal of Symbolic Logic*, vol. XIII (1948), pp. 31–7.

TARKSI, ALFRED. (*LSM*) *Logic, Semantics and Metamathematics*, translated by J. H. Woodger, Oxford, The Clarendon Press, 1956.

——— (*Semantic Truth*) "The Semantic Conception of Truth," *Philosophy and Phenomenological Research*, vol. IV (1944), pp. 341–76. Reprinted in Feigl and Sellars.

——— (*Wahrheitsbegriff*) "Der Wahrheitsbegriff in den formalisierten Sprachen," *Studia Philosophica*, vol. I (1936), pp. 261–405. Translated in *LSM*.

WHITE, MORTON G. (*Dualism*) "The Analytic and Synthetic: an Untenable Dualism," in Sidney Hook (ed.), *John Dewey: Philosopher of Science and Freedom*, New York, Dial Press, 1950, pp. 316–30. Reprinted in Linsky.

WHITEHEAD, A. N., and RUSSELL, BERTRAND. (*PM*) *Principia Mathematica*, 3 vols., Cambridge, Cambridge University Press, 1910–13, 2nd ed., 1925–27.

WILSON, N. L. (*Designation*) "Designation and Description," *Journal of Philosophy*, vol. L (1953), pp. 369–83.

——— (*Existence*) "Existence Assumptions and Contingent Meaningfulness," *Mind*, vol. LXV (1956), pp. 336–45.

——— (*Identity*) "The Identity of Indiscernibles," *Mind*, vol. LXII (1953), pp. 506–11.

——— (*Proper Names*) "In Defense of Proper Names against Descriptions," *Philosophical Studies*, vol. IV (1953), pp. 72–8.

——— (*Property Designation*) "Property Designation and Description," *Philosophical Review*, vol. LXIV (1955), pp. 389–404.

——— (*Space*) "Space, Time, and Individuals," *Journal of Philosophy*, vol. LII (1955), pp. 589–98.

——— (*Rules*) "Symposium: What is a Rule of Language" (with R. M. Martin), *Science, Language and Human Rights* (American Philosophical Association, Eastern Division, vol. I), Philadelphia, University of Pennsylvania Press, 1952.

WITTGENSTEIN, LUDWIG. (*Tractatus*) *Tractatus Logico-Philosophicus*, New York, Harcourt Brace, and London, Kegan Paul, 1922.

Index